SUNDAY MORNING STICKUP

WHAT YOUR PASTOR DOESN'T WANT YOU TO KNOW ABOUT TITHES

A Must – Read for anyone who pays 10% tithes
or gives money to a Leader, Pastor, Charity,
Non-Profit Organization or Church

BY AUTHOR

DAVID LEE

outskirtspress
DENVER, COLORADO

Sunday Morning Stickup
What Your Pastor Doesn't Want You To Know About Tithes
A Must-Read for anyone who pays 10% tithes or gives money to a Leader, Pastor, Charity, Non-Profit Organization or Church
All Rights Reserved.
Copyright © 2013 David Lee
v3.0

Cover Design by David Lee

Outskirts Press, Inc.
http://www.outskirtspress.com

ISBN: 978-1-4327-9164-3

Outskirts Press and the "OP" logo are trademarks belonging to Outskirts Press, Inc.

PRINTED IN THE UNITED STATES OF AMERICA

Special Recognitions

To my beautiful and resourceful wife Renee; The Holy Spirit has used you over the years to balance my perspective concerning His word and His people. Without your significant contribution to my life and gentle, loving encouragement, I would have carried this book in me to my final resting place.

To my brother and sister, whose contribution toward this book has in a momentous way helped to shape its final outcome. Your keen eyes and critical thought processes have helped to clearly convey the message contained within.

To my spiritual father, whose encouraging voice of healing and hope has taught me the importance of embracing my own voice and finding my own path in life based on God's guidance alone. Dad, I am no longer afraid to settle my nerves, clear my throat, and speak His word without apology. Down through the years, it was you who taught me to clearly discern the anointing and voice of God. I owe you a lifetime of thanks and uninhibited gratitude.

This book was given as a gift to

_____

By

_____

On this date in the year of our Lord and Savior Jesus Christ

Table of Contents

Foreword

There is an undertow of frustration finely hidden beneath the delicate fabric of today's Christian experience. We call her Church, the bride of Christ. Forlornly she looks nothing like the church of yesterday. Conflicted in her existence and compromised in her expressions, she bears the name of the Heavenly Father but oftentimes demonstrates the characteristics of His adversary. Although she did not begin this way, today she hurts, wounds, defrauds, and manipulates many who hope to receive healing and help from her hands.

Two thousand years ago, Jesus confronted her leaders and revealed two very significant observations as He stood in her courts, armed with only a whip and passion. *Sunday Morning Stickup* is that whip and passion of today.

Jesus's Public Confrontation
- **Evaluation #1**—My house shall be called a house of prayer
- **Evaluation #2**—You have made it a den of thieves

This accusation, once heralded by the savior in her sacred courts more than two thousand years ago, have manifested themselves into full-blown, undeniable crimes committed in broad daylight. Worst of all, this "stickup" takes place like clockwork, primarily on Sunday mornings.

Star struck, many have given in to larger-than-life personalities and have cast aside the genuine leading of God's Spirit. Talent has taken the place of the true anointing, and it is becoming increasingly difficult for the coming Christian generations to decipher the difference between the two. She (the church) exhibits signs of swelling to the exorbitant totals of ten thousand, twenty thousand, and even thirty thousand-plus members, all gathered together in one place, but real growth escapes her. Her pews are warmed with former members of other churches as opposed to newly converted sinners.

Her sheer size suggests growth and success. To the untrained eye, she looks prosperous. The assumption is made that she must be filled with healthy relationships within. However, the experienced and matured understand the value of thinking deeply as well as critically regarding these matters. They understand that wherever you see swelling, there is generally an infection. To those who are mature and know the way, her growth bears the signs of an unchallenged, unrestrained tumor that is sucking the life of Christ out of the Christian body at an alarming rate.

Smaller churches are unwisely following the flawed pattern of larger ministries when they should be taking their direction from the Father. Many men and women of God are modeling their churches after other men's ministries, when they should be seeking God for His unique plan concerning them and those they lead. What works for one ministry in one city may not work for another in a completely different area. God knows that if this is not dealt with, it has the potential of corrupting the entire body.

The foreknowledge of God has already prescribed that someone be held accountable for the abuse of his people and the exploitation of His holy name.

Just as he performed surgery on the man Adam years ago in the Garden of Eden, so too must the woman—the church—come under the two-edged blade of the creator in the Garden of Modern Day Life.

Judgment Is Inevitable.

The church used to be focused on saving souls. "We are going after souls." That mission statement has been discarded and abandoned as modern day ministry redefines and reestablishes itself throughout the world. She has walked away from talking to sinners on the street corner and has settled for talking to herself behind closed doors at conferences. "And as ye go, preach, saying, the kingdom of heaven is at hand. Heal the sick, cleanse the lepers, raise the dead, cast out devils: freely you have received, freely give" states the Master in *St. Matthew 10:7-8 KJV.* One hundred and fifty dollars to hear the word preached at our powerful conference, "you don't want to miss it", is what we are told. It will cost your church five to ten thousand dollars if you want me to come preach the word to you. The church has lost her focus for souls. She has replaced it with a focus on **OUL ($**atisfying **Our Unrestrained Lust for $**tuff**)**. The term for this is "lasciviousness" and can be found in *St. Jude 1:4.* For deeper insights, your instruction is to read all twenty-five verses.

S T O P

Yes, you must read St. Jude!

The problem we are facing in Christianity today is the vast majority of Christian believers simply take what is said over the pulpit and in books as the gospel truth. They shout "amen" to error and nod their heads in agreement to scriptures that have been twisted and taken out of context. Why? They have stopped reading their Bibles. You must slow down long enough to check the scriptures for yourself in order to validate the truth of the things being spoken to you. I am challenging you to resist the urge to rely on being spoon-fed over the pulpit on Sunday mornings. You can have a deeper understanding of God's word.

He has heard your prayers, and He wants to reveal His word to you in ways that you can truly understand for yourself. In order for this to take place in your life, you must first know that scriptural understanding is tied to scriptural knowledge. Scriptural knowledge isn't enough; God must reveal His word to you. This revelation only comes from the Holy Spirit. In order for you to build a solid understanding of the forthcoming truths revealed in this book, you must do your part by becoming familiar with the scriptures that are referenced within. It is not enough to simply read the words; you must try the spirit of what is said by the Spirit of God and judge the truth of what is written and spoken for yourself. **I am giving instructions that you read the book of St. Jude. It is one chapter long with only twenty-five verses. It is the second to the last book of the Bible, just before the book of Revelation. After you have read it, you may continue.**

If you are unable to read the scriptures now, commit to reading them later. If you agree to do this, you may continue. If you are not willing to do this, do not read any further. Simply return the book.

This book was fourteen years in the making and was not written in an effort to get your money. Neither was it written with the goal of becoming a best seller. That's God's business to decide. I have to confess that the spirit of fear held me captive for all those years. Once God released me from the fear of "what some may say," His words began to consume me. You see I wrote this book out of obedience to a mandate from God on my life. I am doing what I believe in my heart He has asked me to do and I am prepared to stand judgment for this finished work. I believe in it just that much and after reading it so will you. If you have not done what God has instructed you to do because of fear, you are not ready to stand before the judgment seat of Christ. It is important that you obey that voice within you as well. God wants you to know the truth, but above all He wants you to do the truth. It is through knowing and doing the truth, that you are able to firmly plant your feet and knowledgeably take a firm stand for what you know to be right. It is only when you take this stand that you will find true freedom.

As your children read these time-transcending truths one hundred years from now, my prayer is that they find relevance within these passages. I want to encourage you to avoid the temptation of skimming through the pages as you will most assuredly miss the life-changing message contained within. I am asking for your undivided attention. Form your book clubs, get your highlighters, special pens, and bookmarks ready. You must read and reread it again and again. Check the scriptures that are referenced in this book. **For deeper understanding as well as contextual integrity you must read the entire chapter for every scripture referenced herein.** My wife and I along with our mother's did it, so I am not asking you to do something that I have not done myself. Reading the scripture references within and then reading the entire chapter will deepen your understanding of God's word in ways that cannot be explained. It is quite possible that this book will fade with time, but the word of God will stand forever. Do not let your studies end with this book, God wants to reveal his word to you in a very meaningful way.

You will need the following:

- *1 Bible*
- *2 highlighters (different colors), one for highlighting important facts that jumps out to you, and one for highlighting scriptures.*
- *1 special pen*
- *1 bookmark*

Many who love the Christian God are turned off by today's Christian experience. Church attendance is down all throughout Christianity. A recent trending report reveals that there are currently three major monotheistic religions in the world today: Christianity, Islam, and Judaism. These three religions believe in one God. Christianity has the largest number of believers represented by these groups.

In eighty years, the number of Islamic believers will surpass Christian believers. If the trend continues and things keep going in their current direction, the report shows that in 180 years, one half of the world's population will be Islamic (see Christian Chart 1a and Muslim Chart 2b located on pages 68 and 69). One of the major contributors to this trend is the high birth rate among Islamic believers; the other is the fact that they convert more nonbelievers to Islam than Christians do to Christianity. While we say, "Come to my church," they are saying, "Come to my god." It would appear that Christians have strayed from witnessing. When nonbelievers come to our churches, we stick them up with a compelling story about the financial needs of the church and justify these needs by talking about all the family-friendly programs available to them if they would join today. "Give your money to God, so he can release blessings into your life" is normal church lingo nowadays. Oftentimes there is a guaranteed scripted product pitch given over the pulpit, even though no life-changing altar call has been extended. People are encouraged to give their best offering because they owe God (money) for all he has done in their lives. Talks of success, wealth, prosperity, money, going to the next level and even the next dimension fill the pulpit throughout Christianity.

When nonbelievers who are seeking God go to the Muslim mosque, they are presented with a story about their individual need for God, family, and community. They are encouraged to devote their lives to Allah, forsaking all others and to read their Quran. It appears that they have understood one basic, time-transcending truth spoken by the Master who said, *"Wherever a man's treasure is, there will his heart be also." (Matthew 6:21)* If God has your heart, everything else, including your money, will follow.

To state this fact in layman terms, Muslims are focused on souls while Christians are focused on $tuff. A self-centered focus has taken over the North American church as we preach, sing, and shout, "It's MY season," "enlarge MY territory," "money comes to ME now," "go get it... it's YOUR time." We do this while people around us are dying and going to hell. This generation's blood is on our hands. We bear this responsibility collectively. Unless we turn things around and realign our focus to good, old-fashioned Christian principles, that blood will be required of us all on judgment day.

We Are Failing This Generation.

The other major factors contributing to the decline in Christian converts are discussed briefly below. Greater detail is given later in the book. The reality that more Christians simply stay home on Sunday mornings has little to do with the convenience of catching the service electronically. It used to be that sinners would not go to church, but today many Christians do not attend church because they, just like the Savior, are disgusted with what they see taking place in what should be called the house of prayer.

The root cause behind their disconnection with their local church is simple. The preaching has changed. The open vision is fading fast *(1 Samuel 3:1)*. Today's messages of wealth and prosperity are professionally packaged and delivered with polish by motivational speakers standing in the pulpit. The clergy collars have faded, and the once highly respected robes, bearing religious distinction, are discolored and moth-eaten as they hang in the dark, in the back of closets. Alligator shoes, six-figure cars, and seven-figure homes are the new normal as the onlookers who sit in the pews are told,

"You too can have all this and more. You should have it! You deserve to have it! You will have it! Your faith isn't enough though; you must attach a seed to your faith like I did. If you do what I did, you can have what I have. Sow a financial seed, and wait for God's plan to be manifested in your life. Once God gives you the plan for how to be successful, watch the things you are praying for come to pass. Hallelujah glory to God!"

What you should know is that God's plan for the success of your life can never be initiated by any amount of money you will ever give; this includes your tithes. The only thing you can ever give God in order to move Him to bless you abundantly is your life. Your money will never move God. Giving Him your heart will. Your success was initiated by the life that Christ gave for you and to you when he died on the cross more than two thousand years ago. That success is lived out in a life of faith and trust that you give in return to Him.

God gave you Christ; see *St. John 3:16*. If you put your trust in Him by acknowledging Him in all your ways, He will guide you successfully through the uncertainties of life. Chances are you will never be rich, but that is OK, because you will no longer define your success by what you own, drive, wear, live in, or have in your bank account. Neither will you define the success of others by those things. You will define your success by saying yes to God's will alone and doing what He put in your heart to do.

"ConMANlation" is the successful marriage of control and manipulation. It is effectively wielded by those who are in ministry for the money. This results in no one questioning the imbalance of wealth and influence that is prevalent in the church. For all the tithes and sacrificial offerings church members give, they see no relief from their struggles, and no one considers that the gospel is no longer being preached and the church is losing its salt.

Matthew 5:13 (NLT)
You are the salt of the earth. But what good is salt if it has lost its flavor? Can you make it salty again? It will be thrown out and trampled underfoot as worthless.

If you change the message the people are receiving, you change their expectations. When was the last time you heard a message about hell? Humph! When was the last time you heard a message about heaven?

We used to complain about prayer having been taken out of our schools, but I am concerned that the gospel has been taken out of our preaching.

Protect the Brand

Because what some preachers say may negatively impact their "brand," they are careful not to offend. This results in the unadulterated truth being compromised and humanism being preached over our pulpits and in conferences. We seek to be purpose driven, but the Bible instructs us to be Spirit led. Sadly many cannot detect this error as they are in the early stages of being deceived. Fast forward 20 years from now and that deception will be irreversible. The deception is subtle and comes easy, because countless thousands have stopped reading their Bibles for themselves. Not even on Sunday mornings. There is no need to bring their Bibles as the passage is spoon fed to them over jumbo screens. This line of church business does very little to commit the hearer to a lifelong relationship with God. To be more effective, the screens should be turned off all together and the reader's attention redirected to their Bibles. Twenty more years of moving in our current direction and deception will have grown to full maturation so much so that no one will be able to discern what is of God and what is not.

Erroneously, the Christian gaze is affixed on life's jumbo screen and a lifelong relationship with prosperity. The pulpit is projecting the images. The focus used to be "commit to my God, and follow me as I follow Christ." It has been replaced with "Partner with me, and commit to my brand" (even when I preach an entire sermon and do not talk about Christ). Our once crystal clear spiritual focus has degraded, and been replaced with dark specks of worldly similarities, which will one day culminate into political pursuits.

Today's preaching is an HD reflection of this modern day approach to ministry. Today's messages are very different from the preaching we grew up with. I make the distinction between the two because I believe there is a difference between a "message" and "preaching". I would not consider much of what is being spoken over pulpits today as preaching. We are given messages, but what men and women of the cloth were instructed by the apostle Paul to do was preach the Gospel of Jesus Christ. The messages of today can never save the souls of men. It will help them in this life, but it will fail them in the next. It sets the wrong expectations in the hearts of God's people and fails to prepare them for that inevitable accountability meeting, which will assuredly take place in the courts of glory one eternal Sunday morning. You must seek the straight and narrow path.

Matthew 7:13-14 (KJV)
[13] Enter ye in at the strait gate: for wide is the gate, and broad is the way, that leadeth to destruction, and many there be which go in thereat:[14] Because strait is the gate, and narrow is the way, which leadeth unto life, and few there be that find it.

Wrong Focus

Tithing used to be about people. It is now all about the money. *Sunday Morning Stickup* reveals that there are no scriptures that support Christians paying tithes. After embracing this scripturally guided tour through this important subject, you will realize that you do not have to feel guilty about not paying tithes.

It is true; just as many leaders do not feel guilty about living lavishly; you do not have to feel guilty about not tithing. Many who struggle to pay their tithes are often overcome with feelings of guilt and shame. Sometimes you make the decision to pay bills, buy groceries and school clothes for your children, or help someone who is in a financial bind. You are told that doing any of these things in place of paying your 10 percent tithes will provoke God to curse your remaining 90 percent. Deep down inside you say to yourself, "This makes no sense." Good-hearted, generous people live with the fear of "God will curse me if I do not give him his cut."

What you have failed to understand is that God does not want 10 percent of your possessions; He wants to possess 100 percent of you! He knows that once He has 100 percent of you, everything else will follow, up to and including 100 percent of your possessions. There are no limits to what you will give God once you take the limits off your heart to Him.

Does this make sense?

(Highlight or Circle One)
YES / NO / I DO NOT KNOW YET
If your answer is *yes*, keep reading.
If your answer is *no*, keep reading.
If your answer is I do not know yet, keep reading.

For years the preachers would tell us, "If you want to be blessed, you must give God your life." Today that message has been twisted. Messages are now filled with "If you want to be blessed, you must give Him a seed offering" as they take *2 Corinthians 9:6* out of context. To gain the apostle Paul's full counsel on this matter, you must back up to chapter 7 for proper context. Read *2 Corinthians chapters 7, 8 and 9*. If you really want to know the truth for yourself, you have to read.

You have been told that paying tithes is of the utmost importance to being blessed by God. But ask yourself, "What do I really know about tithing?" For most, the only scripture that comes to mind is the one from the book of Malachi. As you ponder this thought, you are beginning to realize that many have talked about tithing and given their testimony about its impacts on their lives, but no one has really ever taken the time to teach you specific truths about it. *Sunday Morning Stickup* will teach you these specific Bible-based truths.

Objective

After reading this book you will be able to answer the following questions:

- What is the true essence of tithing?
- Am I cursed if I do not tithe?
- Does it really take millions of dollars to win souls to Christ?
- Is it OK for the pastor to live lavishly while I struggle with the decisions of paying bills vs. buying food?
- Is church "big business"?
- If my family is in need, do we qualify for assistance from our church?
- Is it OK to use my tithe to help those who are in need?
- Is tithing really required?

Let your journey to liberation begin!
David Lee

Literary Allegory

"I'll never tell your secrets," said the caterpillar to the wise old owl. "I know," said the wise old owl as he proceeded to eat him.

Nearly every pastor knows what I am going to reveal to you in the coming pages. Many simply find it challenging to maintain their current lifestyles without your resources. May the Holy Spirit breathe life into this work and begin the process of freeing you in your mind from what he has already freed you from in your spirit. Upon reading this clear, God-inspired work, I pray that this rightly divided word, spoken in truth and love, will liberate you in your understanding of what God's word has to say about tithing and refocus your heart to align with His word.

I want you to avoid the temptation of skipping past the scripture references contained herein. In order to help you develop a comprehensive understanding, I have included key scriptures throughout this book. You can judge the truth of them for yourself. They are vital to you gaining a deeper perspective of tithes. Before you read any further, I want to ask for your commitment to read each scripture reference and chapter. If you agree, whisper the following under your voice just loud enough so only you can hear it: "I will read every scripture reference and chapter contained in this book."

_____

Your signature

_____

Date

_____

Time

This book is controversial and will forever change how you look at tithing.
Take a deep breath, and let us get started.

CHAPTER 1

You Need Contentment

God does not need your money! Many leaders who have lavish lifestyles are stressed out due to being overextended with financial obligations. The expense of their luxurious homes and cars are compounded with pricey television, radio, and multiple-million-dollar worship facilities. To further complicate the matter, they build facilities that are beyond the operational means of its members. Living beyond their personal means and ministerial resources, they have exhausted their funds, and as a result they have been left with no choice but to pass these expenses on to you. Upon closer inspection of today's sermons and songs, one would have to conclude that leaders are not instructing us to live like we are leaving. To the contrary, sermons and lyrics that encourage "It is your season to be blessed! Just attach a financial seed to your faith, and watch God move on your behalf" have become the focal point of our earthly pursuits, as we take the limits off to gain without constraint this world's possessions.

In the passage below, the apostle Paul provides us with the what's and why's behind our pursuits, as he offers instruction regarding our primary focus as Christian believers.

I John 2:15-17 (NLT)
¹⁵Do not love this world nor the things it offers you, for when
you love the world, you do not have the love of the Father in
you. ¹⁶For the world offers only a craving for physical pleasure,
a craving for everything we see, and pride in our achievements
and possessions. These are not from the Father, but are from this
world. ¹⁷And this world is fading away, along with everything
that people crave. But anyone who does what pleases God will
live forever.

Contentment was once heralded as the premier benchmark of Christian living. "Love not the world, neither the things that are in the world" was once the anthem of those who sought the eternal provisions that do not fade away. *Contentment*—discussions regarding it have all but disappeared from the notes of those who feed the flock of God.

At the root of our discontentment and the rapidly degrading moral social consciousness, can be found the source to why so many individuals are wantonly frustrated. The root-cause simply stated is, the preaching and teaching of God's word has changed. An increased focus on individual accomplishments and the promise of royalty checks has resulted in a drastic shift in the believers' expectations, hence the source of their frustrations. Many of our pastors have fallen in love with money. This love has negatively impacted how they deliver the morning message, the decisions they make concerning church business and how they handle God's people. But every now and then, God will raise up a voice who will without fear declare, "HEY, YOU ARE GOING IN THE WRONG DIRECTION!" A call to action to find balance in today's preaching is needed. We need the kind of balance that will allow us to live modestly in this life, to the extent that it does not circumvent our hope to live eternally in the next.

According to the scriptures, there were three tithes observed by the children of Israel:

1.	A general tithe spoken of in Leviticus 27: 30-33	10 percent
2.	The tithe of the sacred meal with the Levites (Deut 14:22-27)	10 percent
3.	The tithe paid every three years to the poor (Deut. 14:28-29, 26:12-13)	<u>10 percent</u>
		30 percent

While the majority of individuals understand that tithe means "tenth," many do not know that the Israelites gave a separate tenth to address three specific needs. Many theologians agree that they gave as much as 23 to 30 percent tithes. If your pastor only talks about the book of Malachi when discussing tithes but does not teach you the specific requirements outlined in Deuteronomy 14, then you do not fully understand the requirements of tithing and you are not tithing according to the scriptures. I know it is easier to sit in your favorite seat on Sunday morning with your mouth wide open and let someone spoon feed you. I am asking you to stop doing that. Your current and past pastors did not teach you Deuteronomy 14 because they know it is impossible to execute. Do not take my word for it; validate what I am saying by reading Deuteronomy chapter 14 for yourself. Now ask yourself this one simple qualifying question. Can I do what Deuteronomy 14 asks?

Yes | NO

After you have read it, understand that what was written in that passage was never given to the Christian church.

If an individual took the tithes and used them for himself, he was required to get an estimate of what was used and give the value of it as a tithe plus an additional 20 percent. This isn't widely known or talked about on Sunday mornings, but it is in your Bible and you can read it for yourself in Leviticus 27:30-31. In other words, if you fail to give your tithes, according to the law, when you make up your tithes you are supposed to add 1/5th to what you originally owed.

That's right you are supposed to give more than just the original required percentage that you failed to give the first time. If you are not adding 1/5th to the tithe you failed to give, which is an additional 20 percent on top of your original tithe, then you are not tithing according to what God asked for in His law. But I have good news for you; Christians are not required to keep that portion of the Law of Moses.

The scriptures give clear instruction that the Israelites were required to care for:

1. Priests—they did not have an inheritance since they worked in the temple
2. Widows—their husbands (the primary providers) were deceased
3. Strangers—other nations took care of the Israelites when they were wandering as strangers in the wilderness
4. Fatherless—their fathers (the primary providers) were deceased

There are no scriptures where tithes were ever used to spread the Gospel or pay salaries; they were used to care for people. I know many have told you in their own words what God said he wants concerning tithes, but I want you to take a look for yourself at what He actually told Moses He wanted. God gave Moses clear expectations regarding the parameters for tithing. Moses was responsible for cascading God's message down to the people. The message is below.

Leviticus 27:30 (KJV)
And all the tithe of the land, whether of the seed of the land, or
of the fruit of the tree, is the LORD's: it is holy unto the LORD.

Under the old covenant in the Old Testament, the priests were commanded not to work. As a result they could eat of the tithes that the people brought. Under the new covenant in the New Testament, the apostle Paul states, "If a man does not work, he cannot eat." Please pay close attention to the fact that the tithes were eaten. I'll discuss the importance of this a little later in the book.

II Thessalonians 3:8-10 (NLT)
⁸We never accepted food from anyone without paying for it. We
worked hard day and night so we would not be a burden to any
of you. ⁹We certainly had the right to ask you to feed us, but we
wanted to give you an example to follow. ¹⁰Even while we were
with you, we gave you this command: "Those unwilling to work
will not get to eat."

But how was the house of God provided and cared for you may ask? That is a very good question, which is answered in Exodus 30:11-16

Exodus 30:11-16 (KJV)
¹¹ And the LORD spake unto Moses, saying,
¹² When thou takest the sum of the children of Israel after their
number, then shall they give every man a ransom for his soul
unto the LORD, when thou numberest them; that there be no
plague among them, when thou numberest them.
¹³ This they shall give, every one that passeth among them that
are numbered, half a shekel after the shekel of the sanctuary: (a

shekel is twenty gerahs:) an half shekel shall be the offering of the LORD.

14 Every one that passeth among them that are numbered, from twenty years old and above, shall give an offering unto the LORD.

15 The rich shall not give more, and the poor shall not give less than half a shekel, when they give an offering unto the LORD, to make an atonement for your souls.

16 And thou shalt take the atonement money of the children of Israel, and shalt appoint it for the service of the tabernacle of the congregation; that it may be a memorial unto the children of Israel before the LORD, to make an atonement for your souls.

I want to encourage you to read your Bible with understanding. Shekels consisting of gerahs were the money used to care for the temple, not tithes. Some may say well they gave agricultural goods because they did not have money in their day. You are told that money in our day is the replacement of the agricultural goods which were given in Bible days. This simply is not true and there isn't one scripture in the entire Bible to support that line of thinking. After reading the entire 30th chapter of Exodus, you will see for yourself that this simply is not true. Don't take my word for it, read it with your own eyes and pray for understanding!

But how are the priests cared for you may ask? That is a very good question, which is answered in Hebrews 9:15. Since Christ has come and fulfilled the requirements of tithing, we now look to God who has given us all an inheritance in Him. The priests did not work, neither did they have an inheritance; as a result they received tithes from the people. When Jesus Christ died on the cross for all mankind, his death made provisions for an inheritance for everyone, including the priests. Jesus gave them something they did not have before...an inheritance! Since they now have an inheritance, there remains no more need for them to receive tithes from the people. They must now work for what they get and, like the remainder of us who are called the royal priesthood trust God for the rest.

Hebrews 9:15 (NLT)
That is why he is the one who mediates a new covenant between God and people, so that all who are called can receive the eternal inheritance God has promised them. For Christ died to set them free from the penalty of the sins they had committed under that first covenant.

CHAPTER 2

Stick 'Em Up!

In The Book of Acts, when Paul landed in Miletus, he called a meeting with the Elders of Ephesus to meet him there. During that meeting he told them:

> *Acts 20:33-35 (KJV)*
> *³³ I have coveted no man's silver, or gold, or apparel.*
> *³⁴ Yea, ye yourselves know, that these hands have ministered unto my necessities, and to them that were with me.*
> *³⁵ I have shewed you all things, how that so labouring ye ought to support the weak, and to remember the words of the Lord Jesus, how he said, It is more blessed to give than to receive.*

Paul also reminds us that we are not to muzzle the mouths of oxen that tread out corn. The problem is we are seeing an increase in oxen that eat far more corn than they have treaded.

> *1 Timothy 5:18 (KJV)*
> *¹⁸ For the scripture saith, thou shalt not muzzle the ox that treadeth out the corn. And, The labourer is worthy of his reward.*

1 Corinthians 9:7-17 (NLT)

*[7] What soldier has to pay his own expenses? What farmer plants a vineyard and doesn't have the right to **eat some of its fruit?** What shepherd cares for a flock of sheep and isn't allowed to **drink some of the milk?***

[8] Am I expressing merely a human opinion, or does the law say the same thing?

*[9] For the law of Moses says, "You must not muzzle an ox to keep it from **eating as it treads out the grain.**" Was God thinking only about oxen when he said this?*

*[10] Wasn't he actually speaking to us? Yes, it was written for us, so that the one who plows and the one who **threshes the grain** might both expect a **share of the harvest.***

*[11] Since we have **planted spiritual seed** among you, aren't we entitled to a **harvest of physical food and drink?***

[12] If you support others who preach to you, shouldn't we have an even greater right to be supported? But we have never used this right. We would rather put up with anything than be an obstacle to the Good News about Christ.

*[13] Don't you realize that those who work in the temple **get their meals** from the offerings brought to the temple? And those who serve at the altar get a share of the **sacrificial offerings.***

*[14] **In the same way,** the Lord ordered that those who preach the Good News should be supported by those who benefit from it.*

[15] Yet I have never used any of these rights. And I am not writing this to suggest that I want to start now. In fact, I would rather die than lose my right to boast about preaching without charge.

[16] Yet preaching the Good News is not something I can boast about. I am compelled by God to do it. How terrible for me if I didn't preach the Good News!

[17] If I were doing this on my own initiative, I would deserve payment. But I have no choice, for God has given me this sacred trust. [18] What then is my pay? It is the opportunity to preach

the Good News without charging anyone. That's why I never demand my rights when I preach the Good News.

The questions to be answered at this point by those who preach are these:

1. Are you preaching the Good News?
2. Are you compelled by God to preach what you are preaching?
3. Are you preaching of your own initiative?
4. Do you boast about your preaching?
5. Do you preach without charge?

Full-time ministry is not epitomized by quitting one's job and relying solely on other Christians to support you. Stress, strain, and struggle are usually the end result of this kind of thinking. Many have found ways around this by implementing techniques that involve manipulation, guilt, threatening, and instilling fear, while others make promises of great blessings. In the above passages, Paul points out that as a minister, he worked hard because he wanted those he led to learn two vital lessons. The first is that a leader should not be a burden to those he leads. Secondly, a leader should lead by an example that can be easily duplicated. What was the example Paul wanted to pass on to us as Christian believers?

I call them the 13 commandments of preaching

1. Do not preach for money
2. Do not charge people to hear words that cost you nothing
3. Do not manipulate the word
4. Do not be lazy, and do not overtax the people you lead
5. Do not preach on me from the pulpit
6. Preach the truth without compromise

7. You have to do more than just preach
8. Regardless of the position you hold if you want something in life, work for it
9. Preach wherever there is a need and not wherever there is money
10. Study yourself full
11. Think your way clear
12. Pray yourself hot
13. Let yourself go

2Corinthians 11:7-9 (NLT)
⁷ Was I wrong when I humbled myself and honored you by preaching God's Good News to you without expecting anything in return? ⁸ I "robbed" other churches by accepting their contributions so I could serve you at no cost. ⁹ And when I was with you and didn't have enough to live on, I did not become a financial burden to anyone. For the brothers who came from Macedonia brought me all that I needed. I have never been a burden to you, and I never will be.

There are many more scriptures just like this one, and none of them ever asked the children of Israel to bring money as a tithe. The tithes spoken of in Leviticus 27:30 are really not about the land at all. Many have stated that we give money as tithes today because they did not have money in those days. As already stated, this is inaccurate and considered to be an error. They had shekels, gerahs, money, gold, silver, animals, and grain, which they traded based on the temple shekel measurement weight. (See scriptures below.) Although they had it, God never asked for money as a tithe.

Leviticus 27:25
²⁵ And all thy estimations shall be according to the shekel of the sanctuary: twenty gerahs shall be the shekel.

Leviticus 19:35-36 (KJV)
[35] *Ye shall do no unrighteousness in judgment, in meteyard, in weight, or in measure.*
[36] *Just balances, just weights, a just ephah, and a just hin, shall ye have: I* am *the Lord your God, which brought you out of the land of Egypt.*

I Kings 10:29 (NLT)
At that time chariots from Egypt could be purchased for 600 pieces of silver, and horses for 150 pieces of silver.

Hosea 3:1-2 (NLT)
Then the Lord said to me, "Go and love your wife again, even though she commits adultery with another lover. This will illustrate that the Lord still loves Israel, even though the people have turned to other gods and love to worship them."
[2] *So I bought her back for fifteen pieces of silver and five bushels of barley and a measure of wine.* [3] *Then I said to her, "You must live in my house for many days and stop your prostitution. During this time, you will not have sexual relations with anyone, not even with me.*

Leviticus 27:30 (KJV)
And all the tithe of the land, whether of the seed of the land, or of the fruit of the tree, is the LORD's: it is holy unto the LORD.

CHAPTER 3

God Paid the Final Tithe

God kept tithing before His people because later He would reveal to the world a deeper truth concerning its practice. Ultimately He wanted them to understand that the tithes are symbolic of Jesus Christ, who would offer His life on the cross as the living tithe, which God would receive on behalf of humanity. It could be said that the giving of the tithe of Christ's life represented 10 percent of humanity and 100 percent of His own life.

An interesting fact to consider is that the tithe was something that could be eaten or consumed through drinking. When the people gave their tithes, the recipients would consume the tithe and be nourished and sustained of life. In the book of Malachi the people were instructed to bring their tithes to a storehouse. When they needed life sustaining nourishment, they could go to the priest who had the oversight of the storehouse and partake of the tithes which were maintained there. The same people who contributed to stocking the storehouse understood that when the need arose, they could go to the storehouse and have their needs met. Those who hungered could go to the storehouse and find nourishment. The storehouse housed tithes which were consumable goods designed to sustain the people's lives against hunger. Without it many would have died from starvation. We all know the story of Joseph which can be found in Genesis Chapter 41. I want you to pay special attention to verse 56 which references the storehouse. Make note of who benefited from what was housed therein.

Well, the Bible calls Jesus Christ the **Bread of Heaven**, it is through the giving of His tithe life as heaven's bread that all men are able to be sustained so much so that one taste of Him and you will never hunger or thirst again; unlike the tithe of Malachi which the people had to consume often because those tithes could not truly satisfy. Because He is also the **Bread of Life**, one taste of Him and you will live forever *St. John 6:35*. This is why when you accept Him into your heart He gives you eternal life. This is also why God became so angered with the men who were responsible for the oversight of maintaining the tithes, because they corrupted the model/example that God had established. Many of the people brought their tithes faithfully. However, without appropriate leadership management of the tithes, a curse on everyone was inevitable because the leaders represented the people to God. If the government is sick, the people they govern will suffer.

If you decide to tithe, this is a sobering reason why you should care about the integrity of how the money is being handled. What you think you are giving to God may never actually reach Him. It would be like giving your money to your child to pay your electricity bill and he spends it on foolishness. You then become confused as to why flipping the light switch does not produce light in your house. You can't say to the electricity provider, "I paid my bill. I gave the money to my son to take care of it for me. I don't ask any questions I just give him my money. It's not my business what he does with it after that because I wasn't really giving it to him; I was giving it to you, so that's between you and my son". So you continue to flip the switch week after week by giving your tithes but it does not produce the blessings you were anticipating. You refuse to hold your son accountable for his actions because you are blinded by your love for him. Can we at least agree that this is at best the other definition of insanity?

Immortality (the ability to live forever) is obtained when you give up your life which is depleting each passing day and accept Christ into your life. You will be eternally nourished and shall never die if you understand that God does not want to receive the tithe from you, but that He wants to give the tithe to you. The way you receive God's tithe is by giving Him your life. If you have not received Christ into your life, and you are still reading this book, take a quick moment to ask Christ into your heart as Lord and Savior. You do not have to be in a church to do this. You should do it right where you are. Ask him to come into your life now.

St. John 6:51 (KJV)
I am the living bread which came down from heaven: if any man eat of this bread, he shall live for ever: and the bread that I will give is my flesh, which I will give for the life of the world.

The good news is no matter who you are or what you have done, Jesus Christ has already died for you. His dying was the payment of tithes that you and I needed in order for him to provide eternal life to us all. I want to be very clear here. You owe God a debt but Christ paid that tithe debt for you. If you refuse the payment He made on your behalf then you are left with no choice but to pay it for yourself.

Romans 6:23
23 For the wages of sin is death; but the gift of God is eternal life through Jesus Christ our Lord.

The payment for sin including the ones that you commit is death. It does not stop there. Because of your sins, you are supposed to die and spend eternity in hell eternally separated from God. When I say that He died for you, I am really saying you were supposed to die for the sin that was passed on to you from Adam, and for the sins you are committing. The good news of the Gospel is this; God accepted the life of Jesus Christ as payment for your sins and this removed the curse from your life and established the blessing. He willingly died in your place. So if you are looking for a man to love you, Jesus is the only man who can truly give you what you need. He loves you so much that He died for you. Not only did He die for you, He went to hell for you so you do not have to go to hell for yourself. He did all this so that you would not have to die and be eternally separated from God. That is real love and God's plan of provision for you.

In order to take advantage of what Jesus gave, you must accept Him as your Savior from your sin(s), which carries the penalty of death. **All you have to do is repent** (stop doing the things you know to be wrong and start doing right), **ask for forgiveness** (open your mouth, you have to speak the words), **and accept Jesus as the savior who paid the penalty for your sins.** When Jesus gave His life on behalf of mankind, God accepted all humanity (that includes you) via the "tithe" of the life of Jesus Christ. This is the true essence of tithing. Jesus gave God the only tithe God ever truly wanted— His life. That's right, Jesus gave your tithes for you on Calvary. You are on longer obligated to give them for yourself. Jesus Christ is the poured out blessing from the open window of heaven spoken of in the book of Malachi.

In order for God to accept the tithe life of His son, it was necessary for Christ to commit 100 percent of His life to the will of the Father. In like manner, God will accept nothing less from you _____ (insert your name) than the full commitment of your life to Him.

If you want to receive the full benefit that tithing was intended to serve, give Him 100 percent of you, not 10 percent of your money. If He has your heart, your treasure will flow from a heart that recognizes it owes Him everything.

Do you honestly believe that God, who created everything, was hard pressed to receive a smidgen of grain, seed, fruit, and cattle? Do you really believe he was after cows, doves, wheat, barley, mint or money? The hidden agenda of God's master building project has always been and will always be *you*. He fully committed everything committable, just to be one with _____ (insert your name). Jesus funded this master plan with the tithe of His life.

CHAPTER 4

The Tithe Communion Connection

You may have never heard this, but the root cause behind why God required the people to tithe in the past is because he was teaching the world his master plan of redemption.

Today we do not recognize the sacrifice Christ made for all mankind by observing the tithe; we commemorate His sacrifice by observing Communion. The essence of communion in its simplest definition is having a common union in the body of Christ. This common union that all nationalities of people enjoy was made possible through the death, burial and resurrection of Christ. There are no scriptures where Jesus ever paid tithes (money) and He did not ask us to tithe either, but he did ask us to celebrate communion.

Let me ask you a question. Which is better? Not paying tithes or not partaking in Communion? The tithe of Christ made Communion possible. The purpose that His life served was to bring us all into communion with one another and with God. If you tithe every Sunday but do not have communion (common union) with those around you, tithing your money does you no good even if you give 100 percent of it. Read 1 Corinthians

Chapter 13 which talks about love which is an essential element to communion.

In 1 Corinthians 11:27-30 (KJV) the apostle Paul talks about Communion and relationships.

27 Wherefore whosoever shall eat this bread, and drink this cup of the Lord, unworthily, shall be guilty of the body and blood of the Lord.
28 But let a man examine himself, and so let him eat of that bread, and drink of that cup.
29 For he that eateth and drinketh unworthily, eateth and drinketh damnation to himself, not discerning the Lord's body.
30 For this cause many are weak and sickly among you, and many sleep.

Whenever you partake in the act of Communion by consuming the wafer and wine which symbolizes the body and blood of Christ, you are symbolizing outwardly that I am one with the body of Christ. Sickness, weakness and death come on those who are at odds with their brothers and sisters, not recognizing them as fellow believers who are the true body of Christ. If you eat the wafer and drink the wine which represent the body and blood of Christ and only recognize these elements as representative of Him, but fail to recognize that we are His body, you eat and drink damnation to yourself. This is what Paul means in verse 29 when he states ..."not discerning the Lords body. For this cause many are weak and sickly among you, and many die." When you ingest the communion sacraments you are saying outwardly "I am one with Christ's body". If you are divided from those who are in the body of Christ and do not recognize them as a part of the body, you are in essence expressing outwardly a reality that you do not live inwardly. Your participation in Communion then becomes the outward expression of a lie. The reason why so many Christians experience weakness, sickness and sleep (which is death) after taking Communion is because God is allowing them to experience in their own bodies, the weakness, sickness, death and division they are interjecting into the body of Christ. To fix this simply apologize and forgive. We are the body of Christ and the tithe that Christ gave with his life brought unity bonded with peace. To help bring additional clarity read 1 Corinthians chapter 12. Consider this; much of your physical healing will come as you begin to see healing and health in your relationships with those around you, especially with those who are of the household of faith.

Ephesians 4:1-6
4 I therefore, the prisoner of the Lord, beseech you that ye walk worthy of the vocation wherewith ye are called,
² With all lowliness and meekness, with longsuffering, forbearing one another in love;
³ Endeavouring to keep the unity of the Spirit in the bond of peace.
⁴ There is one body, and one Spirit, even as ye are called in one hope of your calling;
⁵ One Lord, one faith, one baptism,
⁶ One God and Father of all, who is above all, and through all, and in you all.

To discern means to perceive a thing for who or what it really is. It is not purely sin that should prevent you from partaking in the communion sacraments; it is division between your brothers and sisters in Christ that Paul is speaking of. Christ came to bring communion between people and God. This is why you cannot so easily walk away from relationships just because you do not agree on a particular issue. Many walk away from Christ centered relationships because they believe an individual may be holding them back from a future filled with success. If God has something for you, not even your enemies can prevent you from having it. But if you walk away from lifelong relationships over petty disagreements or misunderstandings in pursuit of promises, you have misunderstood what Christ came to accomplish through the tithing of His life.

He died, giving his life as the ultimate tithe so that there might be unity in His body. This is a compelling reason why you should not give up on people, and why the church should not be run as a business. Church is not about business relationships, it is about blood relationships. We are blood relatives, made possible only through the blood of Christ. Everybody knows that families sometimes fight. We also know that NO MATTER WHAT family sticks together. The glue that binds us as Christians is the blood of Jesus Christ. If we are divided, our infighting mocks the blood and makes communion laughable.

It is not about the money! What good is a big, beautiful, expensive church filled with people who are faithful tithers but who do not get along? Your division mocks the beauty of your sanctuary and devalues any amount of money that will ever be given. While your church may experience growth, it will struggle to be truly healthy within. The tithe of Christ was about healing those relationships. When pastors replace the message of the cross with a focus on money, they jeopardize every relationship within their sanctuary and frustrate the unity of the Spirit.

Redemption through the blood of Christ is the method whereby God would receive you back into His loving arms. He knew that He could not redeem you through anything from this earth so He sent His Son Jesus, who is the tithe of heaven and earth. When God the Father accepted the sacrificial life of Christ, He was able to fulfill His master plan for humanity: having a personal relationship with you! Theologians call this redemption.

If you give Him 10 percent of your money but never give Him 100 percent of your heart, you have misunderstood the essentials of tithing. I want you to understand that the real purpose tithing was designed to serve was to exemplify the sacrifice of the life of Christ, and position God the Father as the receiver of all mankind. "Whosoever will, let him come" was made possible through the Christ-tithe. I'm trying to tell you that Christ paid your tithes for you on an old rugged cross, on a hill long ago call Calvary; consequently you are no longer required to pay them for yourself. This is what your pastor does not want you to know.

His motivation for giving his life for you had nothing to do with obeying a law. Likewise, your motivation for giving to him should not be based on following any law except the law of love. At the root of all giving is love not law. I could dive deeper and really explore the time-transcending truths of this statement, but I will refrain until later in Chapter 9 when I explain the dynamics of the relationship between Abraham, Lot, and Melchizedek. For now I will simply ask that you read *St. John 3:16* which is the manifestation of God's tithing initiative.

I want to be very clear that the passages of scripture mentioned thus far specifically refer to tithes, not offerings, and **none of these tithes are money.** This is very different from what we do today. Who changed it? If we left off exploring this issue any further, we could conclude from the scriptures previously referenced that we have misunderstood the requirements of tithing. We do not practice it according to how God intended it to be practiced when he gave the requirement to the Israelites. If we have misunderstood this basic fact, that God required as much as 30 percent, my challenge to you is to continue reading. You will become more informed about the remaining facts regarding tithes and how they apply, or should I say do not apply to you.

I want you to be able to speak intelligently when asked:

- "Why are you still blessed even though you do not tithe faithfully?"

- "You only tithe off your net, and I tithe off my gross, so why am I still struggling?"
- "How come I am still struggling and cannot provide for my family even though I tithe?"
- "I am a single mom. My minister lives lavishly while I struggle to provide for my kids. Each week they beg for more money and give more lip service about how they want to see me and my family blessed. They raise two and sometimes three offerings. Should I ask for assistance from my church or personally from my minister, or is there a difference?"
- "The leaders at my church are misappropriating and sometimes stealing the money; should I continue to pay tithes there?"
- "Am I cursed according to Malachi 3:9, or am I blessed according to Galatians 3:9?"

Malachi 3:9 (KJV)
Ye are cursed with a curse: for ye have robbed me, even this whole nation.

Galatians 3:9 (KJV)
So then they which be of faith are blessed with faithful Abraham.

CHAPTER 5

Attitude of Gratitude

The first thing you should know is no amount of tithes you give will ever override poor financial stewardship. Many who tithe faithfully continually experience unimaginable setbacks that keep them in a constant state of struggle. You simply buy things you cannot afford. There is no magic to it and no amount of faith or giving will ever override living beyond your means. Trying to impress people is not wise. If you cannot buy it with cash, there is a good chance you cannot afford it. Many may say, "I use my faith to make up the lack in my life". Paul said, "I can do all things through Christ who strengthens me". What exactly was Paul talking about doing? See the scripture references below.

Philippians 4:12-14 (KJV)
12 I know both how to be abased, and I know how to abound: every where and in all things I am instructed both to be full and to be hungry, both to abound and to suffer need.
13 I can do all things through Christ which strengtheneth me.
14 Notwithstanding ye have well done, that ye did communicate with my affliction.

Now read it in the New Living Translation

Philippians 4:12-14 (NLT)
12 I know how to live on almost nothing or with everything. I have learned the secret of living in every situation, whether it is with a full stomach or empty, with plenty or little. 13 For I can do everything through Christ,[a] who gives me strength. 14 Even so, you have done well to share with me in my present difficulty.

What you have just read is an accurate definition of Christian contentment. Do not be needy. There are those who can afford expensive things, but what many fail to understand is that they are throwing their money away on things that depreciate in value and deplete their wealth. They are broke on another level. At the end of the day, being broke is well, being broke!

For many, although they have given thousands over the years, tithing has not produced so much as a trickle of financial blessing in their lives. Why? The answer is simple. God has everything and needs nothing, not even your tithes.

Psalms 24:1
The earth is the Lord's, and the fulness thereof; the world, and they that dwell therein.

God is more interested in **how** you give than He is in **how much** you give. I am not minimizing the amount of your giving. My emphasis is on the state of your heart when you give. There are other more practical factors to be considered when discussing economic health vs. economic paralysis. There are many experts who have written extensively on this subject, a simple search on the World Wide Web is a good place to start if you need additional information. You can always talk to a financial consultant you trust.

Whatever you give already belongs to Him before you give it. Have you ever considered that God looks at your heart, not your percentage? He evaluates the state of the heart of your giving above the percentage of your giving. In other words He is more likely to accept less from someone who gives it from 100 percent of their heart than He would from someone who gives 10 percent or even 100 percent of what they have but did not really want to give it to Him in the first place.

This should not come as a surprise because many of you are the same way. You and I would rather not receive so much as a glass of water from someone who really did not want us to have it. You may not say it, but you think to yourself. *If you are going to give it with that attitude, I don't want your funky water. Keep it!* The waiter may successfully set the water in front of you, but when you leave the dinner table, the glass is untouched and full with sweat running down the sides. For many, how they felt about the exchange is clearly and purposefully reflected in the tip. How you give is important to God. How you give will inevitably affect what you give.

I believe God feels the same way when we bring our time, talent, or treasure to Him. You want to make every effort to avoid contaminating the gift you bring to God. Knowing this should encourage you because I have just revealed to you the key principle behind being blessed. Regardless of your amount, give from your heart just like Jesus did, and He will gladly receive it. Remember, it's all about your heart and not your percentage.

**God does not want your gift because you "have" to give it.
He accepts it because you "want" to give it.**

In *Philippians 4:19*, the apostle Paul helps us to understand that God will supply all our needs according to his riches in glory by

Christ Jesus. It is also in this same passage that he speaks as a minister who has learned the art of being content with what he has. What Paul does not do is pressure or beg the members of the church of Philippi to give. I included the passage so you can get a better idea of what God intended giving to look like for us today. I want you to pay particular attention to the fact that there is no manipulation, guilt, or pressure and absolutely no begging involved.

Philippians 4:10-20 (NLT)
[10] How I praise the Lord that you are concerned about me again. I know you have always been concerned for me, but you didn't have the chance to help me. [11] Not that I was ever in need, for I have learned how to be content with whatever I have. [12] I know how to live on almost nothing or with everything. I have learned the secret of living in every situation, whether it is with a full stomach or empty, with plenty or little. [13] For I can do everything through Christ, who gives me strength. [14] Even so, you have done well to share with me in my present difficulty.

[15] As you know, you Philippians were the only ones who gave me financial help when I first brought you the Good News and then traveled on from Macedonia. No other church did this. [16] Even when I was in Thessalonica you sent help more than once. [17] I don't say this because I want a gift from you. Rather, I want you to receive a reward for your kindness.

[18] At the moment I have all I need—and more! I am generously supplied with the gifts you sent me with Epaphroditus. They are a sweet-smelling sacrifice that is acceptable and pleasing to God.

[19] And this same God who takes care of me will supply all your needs from his glorious riches, which have been given to us in Christ Jesus.

[20] Now all glory to God our Father forever and ever! Amen.

Under the old covenant, God took care of the needs of those who ministered to his people through a required 10 percent tithe. Today He instructs us to give a freewill offering only. You will notice from the above passage that what the minister received was a gift given out of kindness.

1. It was given in kindness.
2. It was not a requirement because not all the churches gave.
3. There was no preset percentage established that governed the churches then and there is not one now.

The early church understood something that we have failed to comprehend. Tithing was no longer required. This is why there are absolutely no references in the New Testament church of anyone ever paying tithes. When they gave, they did so from their hearts and with great benevolence. They gave to meet needs. They gave so much that the minister stated, "At the moment I have all I need—and more! I am generously supplied with the gifts you sent me with Epaphroditus." Read it again so that you have a clear understanding that *he is not talking about tithes.*

Present-day Christians are instructed in *James 2:15* that if we see someone who is in need (anyone at all), we are to be compassionate and do what is in our power to meet that need. We are asked to open our bowels of mercy and give from our hearts. In the Old Testament, giving was regulated by laws, ordinances, and statutes not love. During that time God wanted them to simply obey the law even if they did not agree with it.

From a hermeneutical standpoint, there is no supporting data in scripture that requires Christians to tithe. If we compare the Mosaic Law to the New Covenant, we will conclude that God has laid no requirements on Christians to tithe at all. Aside from what is preached, it is surprising how little is actually known or understood about the subject.

None of the four references to tithing in the New Testament refer to money: *Matthew 23:23, Luke 11:42, Luke 18:12,* and *Hebrews 7:5.* Each of these passages is making a reference to the law. They do not suggest a predetermined percentage of giving that Christian believers are required to observe. In fact many Christians are unaware that the exact opposite is taught regarding this for New Testament believers. If anyone wants to use the above passages as proof that Christians should tithe, then everyone should be aware that no money ever exchanged hands in any of those passages. They should also be prepared to live by all that the law had commanded. If the apostle Paul was going to talk about Christian tithing requirements, why did he not do so in the seventh chapter of the book of Hebrews where his only discussion about tithes is mentioned? There are 66 books in the Bible. There are 39 in the Old Testament and 27 in the New Testament. Many theologians agree that Paul wrote 14 of the 27 New Testament books; that is more than one half of the New Testament, so why does he not offer one single teaching regarding tithing as a requirement for the church?

Now that you are receiving Bible based teaching about tithes, it is time for a pop quiz. Highlight or circle the answers that make the most scriptural sense?

God wants 10 percent of your money	God wants 100 percent of you
Tithe offerings were money	Tithe offerings were the fruit of the earth
Tithes represent Christ	Tithes represent sowing seeds to be blessed
Tithing is required	Tithing is not required

Take a look at the scripture below regarding the collection of offerings from a local church. You will note first that nothing is said about those church members being required to pay tithes. This is true of the entire New Testament. When Paul talks about giving, he advises the believers that they have to decide for themselves what to give. Their giving is between them and God. He does not stop there, but he brings to their attention that they must first be willing to give; in addition to this, he advises them that the amount they receive is proportionate to the amount they give. Giving and receiving go hand in hand. If you give a little, you will receive a little. If you give a lot, you will receive a lot. Life is cyclical. Everything and every action are connected in some way.

2 Corinthians 9:5-10 (NLT)
⁵ So I thought I should send these brothers ahead of me to make sure the gift you promised is ready. But I want it to be a willing gift, not one given grudgingly.
⁶ Remember this—a farmer who plants only a few seeds will get a small crop. But the one who plants generously will get a generous crop.
⁷ You must each decide in your heart how much to give. And don't give reluctantly or in response to pressure. "For God loves a person who gives cheerfully."
⁸ And God will generously provide all you need. Then you will always have everything you need and plenty left over to share with others.
⁹ As the Scriptures say, "They share freely and give generously to the poor. Their good deeds will be remembered forever."
¹⁰ For God is the one who provides seed for the farmer and then bread to eat. In the same way, he will provide and increase your resources and then produce a great harvest of generosity in you.

This is abundantly clear and really needs no interpretation. What is not so obvious though is that under the old covenant an individual could have given God the full 10 percent of tithes required, and he could do so unwillingly with a grudge. Based on the old covenant, God would have to accept what was brought because that individual fulfilled what was required of him by the law. God had to abide by His own law and receive the disgruntled tithe.

The old covenant gave little consideration for the state of one's heart, only to the success of one's execution of the requirements of the law concerning tithes. To be very clear regarding this point, an individual could be hateful and give the required tithes and still receive the open window, poured out blessing spoken of in the Malachi 3:6-10. It really did not matter how they felt about it as long as they did what God said. He was after their obedience. The new covenant is very different in this respect; God will forgive your disobedience as long as you have a broken spirit and a contrite heart. Since the coming of Christ, you and I are now under the law of liberty which is governed by love. Under this new covenant, you must be careful not to break the law of love. God is looking at your heart.

King David helps us to understand that while men look at your outward deeds, God looks at your heart. Christ has ratified the new covenant through his blood. Ratification means that something is formally approved so it can become valid and implemented. The old way of doing things changed. The New Covenant or New Testament is summed up in this way: no matter who you are or what you have done over the course of your life (good or bad), you can believe your way into a healthy relationship with God. If you say, "Jesus, you are now my Lord and Savior," and then take the ever-so important step of believing in your heart that God raised Jesus from the dead, you will be saved from your sins. You will also gain access to all the benefits of the new covenant which are the blessings that cannot be accessed through giving money.

Hebrews 13:20-21 (NLT)
²⁰ Now may the God of peace who brought up from the dead our Lord Jesus, the great Shepherd of the sheep, and ratified an eternal covenant with his blood
²¹ may he equip you with all you need for doing his will. May he produce in you, through the power of Jesus Christ, every good thing that is pleasing to him. All glory to him forever and ever! Amen.

God looks at our hearts through the law of liberty. God not only judges *what* we do, but he looks at the intent behind *why* we are doing it. What does this mean for us today? If you, just like the widow in the Gospels who gave all she had, do so with a willing heart, it does not matter to God what percentage it is as long as you give it willingly with 100 percent of your heart. You want to be careful that whenever you give anything to God, you do so willingly and with good intentions. Who wants to receive a loaded gift that comes with strings attached or one that is given with a bad attitude?

If you want to experience the manifold blessings of God, give with a good attitude. Whenever you allow someone to coerce you into giving something you really do not want to give, the one who manipulated you into giving it is the only one who receives it. Remember, God looks at your heart and is more inclined to receive a gift given from it.

He will not accept your offering any more than he accepted Cain's. When you give grudgingly, you will receive no return on your investment. Although you may give more than the next person, your offering, just like Cain's offering, will not be received by God. Deep down inside you harbor many compelling reasons why you cannot afford to give to a God who has already given you everything including strength, smarts, ingenuity and favor.

Whatever you give to God already belongs to him even if you do not give it *(I Chronicles 29:14)*. He is looking at your heart! I'm not judging you; I'm trying to help you.

Avoid giving like Cain gave.

Genesis 4:3-5 (NLT)
³ When it was time for the harvest, Cain presented some of his crops as a gift to the Lord.
⁴ Abel also brought a gift—the best of the firstborn lambs from his flock. The Lord ACCEPTED ABEL AND HIS GIFT,
⁵ but he did not accept Cain and his gift. This made Cain very angry, and he looked dejected.

If you want God to bless and receive what you give, I would encourage you to start giving from your heart and not out of a pre-required percentage. When you begin giving out of a grateful heart, you will find that your giving will far exceed 10 percent. The saying, "You can't beat God giving no matter how hard you try" is true. You will never encounter a need that you will not be able to meet because God will favor your offering and most importantly He will favor you.

CHAPTER 6

Going Through the Motions

W hen looking into the Mosaic Law, we understand that it was broken down into three main parts. The parts are as follow:

- **Ceremonial law**—Exclusive to the old covenant. Practicing these laws that were often associated with sacrifices was designed to help the individual identify clean/holy things from unclean/unholy things. We no longer practice these laws because we are now cleansed and made holy through God's son, Jesus Christ. (See *Colossians 2: 8-16*.)
- **Civil law**—Laws that outlined behaviors associated with societal living such as property, inheritance, marriage, and divorce. (See *Leviticus 25:29* for example.) Unlike moral laws, which do not change, civil laws are forever changing. Many government laws today have their roots in these same laws.
- **Moral law**—Twice written in stone because they were being broken while they were being written were the Ten

Commandments *(Exodus 20:2-17)*. They are now written in the hearts of every human being. *(Romans 2:14-15)* Because these laws outline moral behaviors dealing with murder, theft, honesty, adultery, etc., we still observe all these laws (with the exception of the fourth commandment, which required that one of six days be kept holy, that being the Sabbath). See *Colossians 2:14-16* for why we no longer recognize the fourth commandment.

Tithing is associated with ceremonial law. Very simply stated, New Testament believers do not practice ceremonial laws any longer. While we continue to practice many civil and moral laws, it is important to understand that tithing is not associated with either. It is manipulation to make people feel that they are immoral if they do not tithe. Tithing was neither moral nor immoral. Guilt and condemnation are not methods used by the Spirit of God to correct or bring you into the truth of his will for your life.

> *Taken from the NLT:*
> *I Corinthians 2:12 And we have received God's Spirit (not the world's spirit), so we can know the wonderful things God has freely given us.*
> *II Timothy 1:7 For God has not given us a spirit of fear and timidity, but of power...*
> *Romans 8:1 So now there is no condemnation for those who belong to Christ Jesus...*
> *Romans 8:15 So you have not received a spirit that makes you fearful slaves...*

In the one instance where Jesus references tithes, it is in relation to observing the ceremonial law given to Moses, (Remember, the tithe life of Jesus had not yet been given for all humanity).

The story is as follows. Jesus was invited to dinner by one of the religious leaders. He sat down to eat without first washing His hands. Based on the ceremonial law that God had given to Moses, Jesus was supposed to go through a ritual of washings: one before dinner, known as the "first waters" (the Hebrew term is *mayim rishonim*), and one after, known as the "last waters" (the Hebrew term is *mayim aharonim*). He did neither. The idea here is that it was thought that the uncleanliness posed a threat to one's holiness and could bring on poverty as well. Although there is no scripture that specifically states it, it is possible that the origin for the expression "cleanliness is next to godliness" was taken from this tradition. Additionally it was believed that the salt used to preserve food during that time if not washed away after a meal and if rubbed into one's eyes could cause blindness. When the dinner host saw that Jesus did not practice this ceremony, he was stunned!

The man wasted no time expressing his disagreement with Jesus not washing before supper. If you want to be like Jesus, well, you have to get used to people not understanding why you do some of the things you do. If God is leading you, it is better to obey Him than to obey the traditions of men. Jesus was not rattled by this open confrontation, and when you understand God's will regarding something, you have to stand firm on your convictions. Many times we do more harm sparing people's feelings than we do if we simply told them the truth. When Jesus replied to his dinner host, He told him the truth and did not spare his feelings. He talked frankly about tithes. Why? Because Jesus knew that the hearts of the dinner host and his friends were not in the right place regarding this. In fact he calls them greedy and wicked. Jesus was invited to dinner by a man he barely knew and He pronounced judgment on the man and his friends in his own home. It takes real strength to tell the truth in uncomfortable situations. Some of you reading this book are the same way and I applaud your courage.

The idea here is that tithes just like hand washing are governed by ceremonial laws, which according to Colossians 2 are no longer observed by Christians. These laws and ordinances have been nailed to the cross of Christ and have been taken out of our way.

Luke 11:37-42 (NLT)
[37] As Jesus was speaking, one of the Pharisees invited him home for a meal. So he went in and took his place at the table.
[38] His host was amazed to see that he sat down to eat without first performing the hand-washing ceremony required by Jewish custom.
[39] Then the Lord said to him, "You Pharisees are so careful to clean the outside of the cup and the dish, but inside you are filthy—full of greed and wickedness!
[40] Fools! Didn't God make the inside as well as the outside?
[41] So clean the inside by giving gifts to the poor, and you will be clean all over.
[42] "What sorrow awaits you Pharisees! For you are careful to tithe even the tiniest income from your herb gardens, but you ignore justice and the love of God. You should tithe, yes, but do not neglect the more important things.

When Jesus tells him that he should tithe, He is right because Jesus had not died yet. The ceremonial law that required the man to tithe had not yet been nailed to Christ's cross. Here, the scripture reference states that the ordinances of the law have been taken out of our way and nailed to His cross since Christ's death and resurrection.

Colossians 2:14 (KJV)
Blotting out the handwriting of ordinances that was against us, which was contrary to us, and took it out of the way, nailing it to the cross...

There is a lot going on in the previously mentioned passage that you should be aware of. I however, want to draw your attention to four very important facts regarding Jesus's dinner.

- Fact #1: Jesus accused them of having the wrong focus. They wanted to look clean and holy outwardly based on what would be the equivalent of today's suits, ties, alligator shoes, fine homes, and cars. Jesus exposes their real motives when he calls them greedy and wicked. Jesus says to them, all the things you have make you look successful and holy, but the real truth is those things were acquired through greed and wickedness.
- Fact #2: Jesus tells them that genuine cleanliness in God's eyes is when you love people and help those who are in need. Helping those in need was the basis of tithing. It was not intended to be used to pay mortgages, light bills, and staff salaries or to send your leader's kids to private schools or purchase private jets.
- Fact #3: They did not tithe money. The tithes they gave were from their gardens. They had plenty of wealth, yet they tithed out of their produce, because they understood that this is what the law required.
- Fact #4: Jesus is speaking to the Jews regarding a tithe requirement that was given only to the Jews based on the Mosaic Law.

This is important because the Mosaic Law was never given to Gentiles. Jesus says to the Jewish leader, "*You* should tithe, yes..." This statement was never spoken to anyone of non-Jewish descent.

Jesus knew that He was the only tithe that God ever wanted; this is why there are no recorded instances in the entire Bible where you ever see him paying tithes. Christ was thirty years old when John the Baptist stated "Behold the Lamb of God, who takes away the sin of the world." (John 1:29 KJV) Make no mistake about it, he would freely and willingly give his life as *the* tithe for humanity.

God had intricately woven tithing into the cultural fabric of the Jewish nation. He was forever establishing the idea with them that the sacrifice of one would bless many.

Let me explain.

If a Jewish person had ten lambs, God required that one of those lambs be given to Him. When God accepted the life of the one sacrificial lamb, He was in essence accepting all ten. The one lamb that God accepted represented His acceptance and blessing of the remaining nine. Well, it's not just that Jesus is the lamb of God; He is *the* tithe that God really needed to make it possible for Him to implement the plan of salvation for all men! I want to stress again that it is worth knowing that when the scriptures speak of tithing, it is not in reference to money. For a clearer understanding on Jesus being the only tithe that God really wanted, read Hebrew chapters seven through ten.

Jesus called the religious leaders greedy preachers! He said that these leaders put more emphasis on tithes than they did making sure the people they led were taken care of. He accused them of being unjust and not truly expressing the love of God. There are several types of leaders described in the scriptures. In the next chapter I want to focus on two: the Good Shepherd and the Hireling.

CHAPTER 7

Greedy Preachers

I want to commend every pastor who has resisted the influence of the world from coming into your church. I celebrate you and give you flowers now and say thank you for sacrificing your life to ensure those whom you lead are fed the word of God and remain untainted by the world's influence. You may never be recognized by the higher echelon of life. They may never give you a prestigious award and you many never have your face shown on a television broadcast, or have an article written about you in a fancy magazine. Although you have a powerful word in your mouth, you are overlooked and never receive the validation of men by receiving a call or letter, informing you that they want you to preach at their conference. You think we don't know you but nothing could be farther from the truth. You know who you are, and so do we. More importantly, God knows you. When He comes to make up his jewels, you will join Him in eternity and you shall wear a soul winner's crown. We love this kind of pastor! My prayer is that you have unlimited resources at your disposal in order to meet the needs of the people you lead and win back the lost sheep.

Jesus gives us an understanding of what a good shepherd is. In the tenth chapter of the book of St. John, He helps us understand the difference between pastors who are in it for souls vs. those who are in it for the money.

St. John 10:7-15 (KJV)
[7] Then said Jesus unto them again, Verily, verily, I say unto you, I am the door of the sheep.
[8] All that ever came before me are thieves and robbers: but the sheep did not hear them.
[9] I am the door: by me if any man enter in, he shall be saved, and shall go in and out, and find pasture.
[10] The thief cometh not, but for to steal, and to kill, and to destroy: I am come that they might have life, and that they might have it more abundantly.
[11] I am the good shepherd: the good shepherd giveth his life for the sheep.
[12] But he that is an hireling, and not the shepherd, whose own the sheep are not, seeth the wolf coming, and leaveth the sheep, and fleeth: and the wolf catcheth them, and scattereth the sheep.
[13] The hireling fleeth, because he is an hireling, and careth not for the sheep.
[14] I am the good shepherd, and know my sheep, and am known of mine.
[15] As the Father knoweth me, even so know I the Father: and I lay down my life for the sheep.

The Good Shepherd

1. **Points the people to Christ and not to himself (St. John 10:7)**
He avoids lording over the people as though he were their God. Through his actions, he earns the ability to be honored by the people he leads. He knows that honor has to be earned not taught. He knows that when the people he leads sense that

his love for them is genuine; the ways in which they will honor him will be limitless. Wisely he redirects this honor to Christ.

2. **He avoids putting a yoke on the necks of the people by keeping tabs on their every move. (St. John 10:9)**
A good shepherd does not keep tabs on the whereabouts of his members. He knows that anyone who is supposed to be under his care will be there in response to a mandate placed deep within them from God. In addition to this he is not insecure or intimidated by younger, gifted preachers who serve with him.

He does not discourage any member who decides to leave his church. His members are accountable and committed in response to the love God has shown them. As a result, he does not have to invest time in a system that keeps him informed about where everybody is. He knows they are there out of a genuine commitment to something or someone much bigger than him. He understands these types of systems stunt the growth of his church.

3. **Sacrifices his life for the sheep (St. John 10:11)**
He has to find balance because of how much he cares for the people he leads. Oftentimes he puts the needs of his church before his own family and his own needs. He spends countless hours preparing himself by studying the word of God to show himself approved so that he can deliver a soul winning sermon to his congregation. He falls asleep with the Bible on his chest. He never studies to belittle or publicly humiliate because he understands that these things break trust. He defends the Gospel with his life. He will never leave nor forsake those he leads. As the people see him sacrificing, they will in turn freely do the same.

The Hireling

It's important to know that Jesus defines the hireling as a thief and a robber who has come to kill, steal, and destroy. Most individuals believe Jesus is describing the enemy (Satan). He is not. Jesus is describing a comparison between a good shepherd and a hireling. See St. John 10:10

The hireling thieves who have come to kill, steal, and destroy are really preachers who preach for money. These are the wolves in sheep's clothing the Bible warns about.

He moves from one church to another looking for better opportunities. He does not understand that each move is actually demotional judgment from God. Because he is in it for the money, he ignores any voice of reason (internal or external) that threatens his promotion or profits. He generally does not study to feed the sheep. His preaching is primarily reactionary. Because his messages are not spirit led, you can always tell what is going on in the hireling's life or in the ministry based on the message he preaches.

Looking Glass – Wolf in Sheep's Clothing

"I came to get God's money," he says, as he brandishes his $3,500 diamond-studded wristwatch. Modestly hidden behind his monogrammed custom shirt are three-hundred-dollar, diamond-studded cuffed links. Most of the people who are pledging their rent and medicine money toward the new church building project, do not notice. Make no mistake about it; he is in it for the money. He unleashes on the congregation, "If you don't like it, there's the door!" A woman and her two children who are there for the first time take him up on his offer and leave. He beats his chest, his eyes crinkle, as he peers across the congregation. Passionately he thunders, "I am the voice of God; don't you listen to anybody other than me. Anybody who tries to tell you that God has a word for you is a snake!" He pounds on his chest harder and roars, "God only speaks through me, period!" Gasping for air, he rests on the podium beckoning for someone to bring him water and a towel to wipe the sweat from his brow. He peers deeply, more purposefully across the room once again intimidating the onlookers. Like the dropping of a soft blanket, a reverent silence has settled over the room. Taking a deep breath, he states, "I ain't scared of none of you! If you don't like it, take it up with God. My authority comes from Him, so don't give me no lip. You will do it my way, or you will get out of here!"

Now you may be asking yourself, "What is wrong with this guy and why does he create such a threatening and hostile environment?"

The answer is simple: ...he careth not for the sheep. *(St. John 10:13)*

He does not have time to care about the needs of the people because he is trying to build a church. He is not interested in building people; he is interested in controlling them. He is in it for the money! Like a bull in a fragile fine china store he is a triple threat; reckless, abusive and in a position of authority. When the wicked are in charge, the people are oppressed.

Proverbs 29:2 (KJV)
When the righteous are in authority, the people rejoice: but when the wicked beareth rule, the people mourn.

Proverbs 28:15 (KJV)
As a roaring lion, and a ranging bear; so is a wicked ruler over the poor people.

He is in an enlarged place, yet he operates from a mom-and-pop perspective. This explains why he appears to be void of wisdom. Just as fast as new members join, he runs twice as many off. He will never erect a thriving vibrant church of many nationalities. His ministry is one of revolving doors and limited commitments within. There is as much turn over in his leadership ranks as there is at the agent level within call centers. Ultimately, he will only be surrounded by weak leaders who lack the spiritual maturity to hold him accountable for poor ecumenical oversight. Why do you think he runs off anyone who is seasoned in the word? His ministry style attracts those who are drawn to abuse, and he doles it out on a weekly basis unchallenged. One not-so-obvious problem with his behavior is that he is teaching by example. I believe people reproduce what they see produced. As a result he is raising more in ministry who will walk in his ways. The shadow he casts as a leader is fifty shades darker than most. If you check his past, you will find that it is filled with years of abuse and broken relationships.

- He talks about the word of God, but he is not an avid studier.
- He preaches other people's messages and claims them as his own.
- He preaches to address issues; as a result his messages are purely reactionary.
- He wields and manipulates the word of God to control anyone who threatens his position, promotion, or profits (he practices conmanlation).
- He constantly tears down what has been built up.
- He loses as many followers as he gains.
- He places only his family in key decision-making positions; it's his way of maintaining control.
- His life demonstrates a lack of self-restraint physically, relationally, and emotionally.

- He publicly castrates anyone he feels threatens or questions his system of control.
- He believes control and wealth go hand in hand.
- He does not meet with his leaders to provide fiscal or organizational direction because he does not feel that he has to. Only he knows what's going on.
- He has time on his schedule for preaching engagements, but refuses offers from churches he considers to be C & D class ministries (who only have a small membership and cannot pay him the minimum required fee to preach).
- He does not take calls from, spend quality time with, or schedule counseling sessions with his own members. He justifies this by pointing to his busy schedule, deferring this work to those who surround him.
- He has thousands of members, but he does not genuinely know one dozen of them, nor does he care to know his leadership team by name. His knowledge of them goes no further than face recognition. He likes it this way as this approach makes it easier for him to get rid of those who do not do things his way.
- He is not open to suggestions.
- His lips are wet from the unrestrained use of profanity
- He preaches for money.

The scriptures help us understand the root cause behind why he exemplifies these behaviors. He is in the people business; however, he does not genuinely care for people. He is preoccupied with caring for his own. To do this he must be the product champion of his own brand of control and manipulation. I call it conmanlation. It is the successful execution of CONtrol and MANipuLATION.

- **Conmanlation**—to be the subject matter expert of one's own brand of control and manipulation.

Looking Glass – Stick 'Em Up

"You have no integrity, you cannot be trusted and God cannot bless you! I mean you are a robber and a thief. If you think you are going to heaven, you are fooling yourself. God isn't going to let you into His kingdom." She is visibly drenched as sweat drips from the armpits and the upper middle back of her $1,700 Nina Ricci suit that she caught on sale while preaching on the East Coast this past Thursday. "If you are not a tither, you cannot serve in this church," she continues. "I don't even want you playing an instrument or singing to me because you have nothing to offer that's worth hearing, and I know God doesn't want any praise from a joker who has the audacity to rob him. In fact if you are sitting beside someone who is not standing with a tithe envelope in their hand, ask that person, are you a thief?" She instructs them to "wait for an answer." "If they don't answer you, move your seat because I don't want that curse that's on them to get on you." She kicks off her $1,600 Jimmy Choo "Esam" Crystal Heel Platform Pumps and instructs the tithers to bring their tithes and "lay them up here on this altar under the soles of my shoes because there's a blessing on my feet." The envelopes begin to pile up as the newly polished, pink and powder blue shoes slowly disappear under the countless array of envelopes. "Step into the anointing while God is blessing," she instructs.

Looking Glass – Help My Family

A young man in his mid-thirties slowly makes his way down the aisle. He is clean cut and conservatively dressed: khaki trousers, a freshly pressed white oxford shirt, and no tie. He has poorly polished, dark brown Bostonian shoes, which he didn't have time to polish because he was running late due to getting his two boys who are five and six years old, along with their eight-year-old sister, ready for church this morning. "All these aisles lead to Jesus," states the preacher as dozens make their way to the front of the sanctuary. Tears are streaming uncontrollably down his face. As he approaches, one of the ministers eagerly awaits with both hands outstretched to receive him. "What brought you to the altar today, sir?" the minister asks.

His face is wet from the endless flow of tears, but he pushes them back, wiping each cheek aggressively with the sleeve of his white shirt as though the tears were an intrusion. The children stand in confusion wondering, "What's the matter with daddy?" For months he had done a good job of hiding his struggle from his children. He is an out of work single father, but today something was different. Something that he could not explain was happening to him. His life would never be the same again. The youngest boy clutches his father's left leg tightly, and although the usher is trying to pull him away, she is unsuccessful. The child will not budge.

The minister takes him by both hands. He slowly lifts his head, peering through the glistening onslaught of salty tears. The man fixes his eyes on the older gentleman who has engaged him in dialogue. Somewhat embarrassed by his overwhelming display of emotional paralysis, he stammers illegibly, "I love God and could really use some help." The sound of the singing coming through the state of the art sound system is so loud that it makes it a challenge for the older gentleman to make out exactly what the young man has said...so he asks again. "Tell me again son why you have come today?" Clearing his throat, the young man takes a very deep staggering breath as he tries to regain his composure. Realizing that he has to compete with the loud base speaker sitting twelve feet away he's ready to speak louder. The minister seeks for a firmer grip as he squeezes his hands and leans in closer, being careful not to misunderstand a second time. The young man's heart is heavy. His arms feel like they weigh a ton and his knees are buckling, but somehow he made it to the altar. His struggle is visible, but the two men are connected. He senses that maybe these ministers can at least pray for him and point him in the right direction.

Broken and drawn out by the heartfelt, soul-piercing sermon he has just heard about God supplying your need, he takes advantage of the window of opportunity to bare his soul and tell the minister all about his struggle. The altar is full. The minister's training tells him to pray and move on quickly to the next person who has come, but he is well seasoned and aptly experienced as a man of the cloth. He has a sense that he must maintain this connection and pray this man through. The minister understands that the outward expressions of turmoil are but a reflection of the hidden inner struggle taking place deep within the man's soul. He understands that he has to balance the allotment of time given him to pray fervently and effectively, because in ten minutes the altar is going to be completely empty giving way to the order of service. The only thing left will be the issues of those who were able to quickly lay down their burdens at the feet of Jesus in that brief ten-minute moment.

Laboring over souls is a lost concept to this generation of believers. The idea of tarrying with individuals and holding on to the horns of the altar, until a life-changing breakthrough happens in the life of the one who has come to the altar, seeking deliverance from God is rarely ever seen any more in our churches. In their meetings ministers are told, "You are not that anointed, so don't be laying hands on people's heads and praying hard for them. Hold their hands when you pray. We only have ten minutes, so find out what they need, pray and move on to the next one. Do not labor with those who come to the altar because we don't have time. All we need you to do is pray and that's it". We used to cast the devil out and pray until people got their breakthrough. It would appear that we have gradually settled on providing the devil with a security detail, priority parking, and elevated seating complete with a chair that looks more like a throne.

The minister chooses his words carefully, explaining to the man that God can and will supply all his needs according to the riches God has at his disposal in heaven.

Suddenly, the change in music is the gentle queue that the order of service is about to change and his ten minutes are up. Obediently the minister cuts it short and concludes his prayer and prepares to return to his seat. Neither the minister nor the Spirit are finished working with the man, but the minister quenches the Spirit because he does not want to cause any waves. He faithfully obeys the order of the house and wraps up his prayer and quietly returns to his seat. Another preacher—young, polished, and good looking with a clean cut and blond highlight spikes in his hair takes the microphone and charismatically urges the people to "quickly, quickly, quickly, dig deep and give God your best offering. Everyone get a $213 offering and sow into your 2013 year of prosperity and abundance. If you want to be blessed, you have to sow a seed. You've got to move now while the Spirit is moving. Don't think! Just trust God." The blinding sparkle from the sixteen-diamond-studded pinky ring gleams periodically as he holds the microphone in his left hand. The young father is unable to participate in the giving. Despite his degree in economics, he has been unemployed for the past six months and counting.

No one notices, but the thirteen-year-old girl sitting in the third seat of the middle row has timed the altar call. Thirteen minutes total for the entire exercise from start to finish. The second offering totaled twenty six minutes. As if she was moving in slow motion, her demeanor changes. She ponders the following thought deeply within as she shrinks back in her chair, folding her arms tightly across her chest. "Does anyone notice that there seems to be plenty of time to collect the money but very little time dedicated to laboring with hurting people?" Her pondering gives way to deep thought as dissatisfaction starts to settle in. "Bera! Sit up straight in that chair," her mother scolds.

The paradigm shift ushers her into a moment of clarity. She wonders, "Why can't there be a second altar call just like there is a second offering?"

Obedient to the instructions he has just been given by the preacher, the man borrows ten dollars from the slightly mature, nicely dressed woman sitting beside his eight-year-old daughter whose name is Birsha. His offering envelope is completely filled out, and he is careful to ensure there are no dog ears or folds on the ten-dollar bill. It's only ten dollars, but as a trained economist he has always handled money responsibly. He also believes God is a king who looks at his heart, so it is important to him to present his best, no matter the amount. Waving his envelop and holding it high as the preacher has instructed, he cannot help but peek around. He notices all the people who have their hands raised with money in them. This single father begins to question the following deeply within. "What do you do when you feel like your faith has been pricked and your pocket picked at the same time? Why do I feel like I am being stuck up this Sunday morning especially considering I really did not get what I came for?" He is in the early stages of a monumental change which will take place on the political scene in the foreseeable future with how money will be handled in ministry. Unknown to him, the role he will play will be significant.

CHAPTER 8

Tithing: God's Welfare System

Welfare is a governmental agency that provides funds and aid to people in need, especially those *unable* to work. In the end, this term replaces "charity" as it was known for thousands of years, being the act of providing for those who temporarily or permanently could not provide for themselves.

Whether we are talking about a democracy which is government of the people, by the people as defined by Lincoln during his Gettysburg address on November 19, 1863; or a theocracy which is a form of government in which God is officially recognized as the civil ruler. In both cases it is the responsibility of the one(s) in charge to ensure that those for whom they have been given the oversight are properly provided and cared for. All you have to do is study history, and it will teach you that the social welfare system can be dated as far back as the Roman Empire. During that time the poor were helped by the Caesar Trajan. History also reveals that the US, under the Presidential leadership of Franklin D. Roosevelt, organized its first welfare initiative during the time of the Great Depression, which started October 24, 1929. While the US welfare system has undergone many reforms and revisions, at the foundation of its existence is the unabridged focus to help those who are in need, whether that help be long or short term in its existence.

Tithing, in its purest existence has at its core the basic fundamental purpose of ensuring the needs of people were not purposefully ignored or innocently overlooked. A foundational understanding of tithing is that it was God's welfare system. It was God's way of ensuring there were provisions readily available to meet the needs of anyone and everyone who was under his care. It was God's insurance policy against Him being labeled "a deadbeat dad."

CHAPTER 9

Mission Impossible - I Did It Because I Love You

There are no recorded instances where Abraham paid tithes as a lifelong practice. Abraham gave tithes to Melchizedek as a onetime event. No one ever told you this, and I felt that it was important that you knew this important fact. If this is the scriptural example that pastors use as a model for giving tithes, I would be more than happy to tithe as Abraham did. Abraham tithed once! No record is shared in the scriptures anywhere else where Abraham practiced a lifestyle of giving tithes. I realize that you may not know much of what has been revealed thus far. Now that you know, you are responsible for responding to the truth. How should you respond? One good way is by informing others so that they no longer live in ignorance of what God's word really teaches about tithes. If your pastor is reading this book, he or she now knows as well. If you believe they do not know provide them with their own copy of this book. Do not give them yours since there are personal exercises included related specifically to you including a 1 year follow up. Do not withhold the truth of God's word from them as so many have done to you.

Abraham was wealthy.

Genesis 13:2 (KJV)
And Abram was very rich in cattle, in silver, and in gold.

Remember your commitment to read all the scriptures. If you skipped reading Genesis chapter 13, back up and read it before continuing.

The chapter you have just read is a high-level overview of Abraham's wealth. He had this long before he gave any tithes. He did not acquire blessings as a result of giving tithes. Abraham was extremely wealthy because he obeyed God. This took place before he met Melchizedek. When he gave Melchizedek tithes, he did not do so out of the wealth contained in Genesis chapter 13. This is important. He did not give tithes out of his possessions. He gave tithes out of his repossessions! He did not pay tithes out of his possessions. He paid tithes out of his repossessions! In fact, *Genesis 14:18-20* reveals that Melchizedek gave Abraham a blessing before receiving tithes from him. This is something that most people who read the Holy Scriptures overlook. Exegesis is a word that is thrown around quite frequently. It is a Greek word that means to draw out. Eisegesis is the opposite of exegesis, and it means to draw in.

I have included a pronunciation key for your convenience:

- Exegesis: pronounced [ek-si-jee-sis]—{ek-see-gee-sis}/
- Eisegesis: pronounced [ahy-si-jee-sis]—{eye-see-gee-sis}

Exegesis would be the equivalent of telling a story exactly as it was told to you. **Eisegesis** is the equivalent of telling a story that was told to you but with your own spin, giving it a different meaning than what the original person who told it to you had in mind. I think you know where I'm going with this. You guessed it; many leaders have given you an eisegesis explanation of tithing. As a result they have misinformed you about the subject based on God's original intent. I have included scriptures throughout this book and encourage you to follow up with reading them so you will solidify for yourself what the Bible actually says. Why is this significant? It is important that you begin reading your Bible so that you know what it says. Don't be an SMSFC, Sunday Morning, Spoon-Fed Christian. Christians like that are easy prey for hirelings. You should already begin to realize how misunderstanding tithes and the purpose they were designed to serve have led to errors, feelings of guilt, manipulation, and a gross imbalance of provisions in the church. Everyone can see it. It is time for you to do something about it.

FACT:
Abraham gave Melchizedek tithes from the spoils he had taken in battle. He was already a wealthy man without the tithe. Scripture does not record where he ever gave tithes out of his own personal possessions.

Here is the background story that led up to the moment when Abraham gave tithes to Melchizedek. Genesis 13 KJV begins with, *"And Abram went up out of Egypt, he, and his wife, and all that he had, and Lot with him, into the south. And Abram was very rich in cattle, in silver, and in gold."* The significance of this will come into play as we explore Abraham's encounter with Melchizedek in a moment. It is important to note here that Abraham was so wealthy that he had to part ways with his nephew Lot. Their combined accumulated wealth made it necessary for Abraham and Lot to implement a geographical separation. They would never experience relational separation. Their separation was a business decision that involved expansion. It was not a split over wealth.

Lot ultimately became a prisoner of war. When Abraham heard about the misfortune that had happened to his nephew, he mobilized his army to go and get him back. The rescue of Lot set the stage for Abraham's encounter with Melchizedek. The men who took Lot prisoner also took the wealth of the city in which Lot lived. They took the wealth of both Sodom and Gomorrah. From a business standpoint, it would have made sense for Abraham to fight against the men who stole all these riches along with his nephew. If he was successful in battle, not only could he have re- deemed Lot but he could also become an even wealthier man by taking possession of all the recovered loot.

When Abraham mobilized his army, he did not consider the wealth that could be gained. He was not on a labor of loot. Abraham was on a labor of love. He is one of the best examples of what church leadership should look like when it comes to min- istry and money. Primarily he viewed his ministry/mission as an opportunity to save a life, not to get rich. He left the ninety-nine to rescue one because one saved soul was just that important to him. You always have been and always will be God's primary fo- cus in ministry. Any church that does not have winning the lost at the helm of its focus is not about the Father's business. When Abraham made the decision to engage the enemy in battle; I am sure he thought to himself it was an impossible mission consid- ering the number of men he had with him. Four kings against one man and a very small volunteer army! Some things have to be done regardless of the odds. Because his story was a typol- ogy of what Christ would ultimately do for sinners, Abraham found success in his recovery campaign. God give us pastors who will against all odds, engage the enemy in battle on our behalf. Fighting Shepherds who fight the devil and not people!

Abraham was able to redeem the life of his nephew. The con- fiscated loot was just a bonus, not the primary focus. Since he put up the investment needed to launch this military campaign, anything he seized in battle rightfully became his to claim. I want to show you the balanced decision making that Abraham demonstrated when it came to ministry and money. I have in- cluded the account below.

1. Abraham gave Melchizedek a tenth of the goods that were repossessed. He gave nothing of his own personal possessions. It's important to note that his wealth was not contingent upon giving tithes. The window had already been opened, and the blessing poured out on his life. Abraham was loaded before he gave Melchizedek a dime.

2. Abraham did not keep any of the repossessions for himself. Because he was already rich, he knew that if he had kept the recovered wealth, the king of Sodom from whom they were originally stolen would say that Abraham was made rich because of the repossessions he kept.

3. Abraham did not pay the guys who went to battle with him out of his own personal wealth. He paid them out of what was recovered.

I want you to pay attention to the fact that the King of Sodom tried to strike a deal with Abraham by telling him to give the people back and just keep the money. Today these men and women who really are not pastors have traded their congregations in for the money. It seems that they have made a deal with the devil by selling the people out for fame and exorbitant fortunes. This is why they have no relationship with those they pastor, but only a select few. They tell themselves that "when you reach this level of ministry, everything changes and you can never pastor the way you used to ever again". If your son is in trouble, do not look for this pastor to walk through the front door of your home and help you fight for him. He will send a representative to fight on his behalf because he is busy. He is more of a pulpiteer than a pastor.

I define a pulpiteer as someone who pastors a church but sends someone else to carry out his or her pastoral duties. Pulpiteers consider these duties grunt work and would never

be caught fellowshipping on a common level with us. Do not expect a relationship with him outside of Sunday Morning.

In this passage, Abraham does not give anyone anything out of his own pockets, not even the 318 guys who helped him. He is not being selfish. You are not witnessing the antics of a shrewd businessman either. The reason he behaves this way is because this story for him is not about recovering wealth; it was about redeeming the life of the one person he loved deeply. Abraham had no children and Lot had no father so they shared a special bond that few can understand. Lot was imperfect, made bad decisions and hung out with people whose lifestyles were less than regal but he had one thing going for him. He had an uncle (kinsman) who wanted him back (imperfections and all) no matter what. You see, Abraham knew Lot had flaws before he decided to commit himself to helping him. He spared no expense when it came to getting his nephew out of trouble. Lot's father, Haran, was dead. Abraham took his responsibility as protector in the life of Lot very seriously and his love for Lot was irrevocable. He loved Lot so much that he was willing to take on 4 powerful conquering kings in order to rescue him. It was an impossible mission and he would have to put his life on the line in this initiative, but his motivation was love. When you are motivated by love you can accomplish anything. I want to challenge you to love people.

Lot had made some bad choices, but this did not diminish Abraham's commitment toward him as a surrogate father. It is from this place of personal dedication that Abraham took no one with him into this recovery effort that was in it for the money.

Many people stay away from church because they believe the preacher is money hungry. Based on many of today's examples, it's hard to convince them otherwise. They have a hard time understanding how a preacher can drive up in a Bentley while he has elderly church members who struggle with their monthly ritual of "Do I buy food, do I buy medicine, or should I pay bills?" They don't understand how the leader can go out to eat after Sunday morning service and splurge on his family and their exclusive circle of friends (none of which are regular church members) to the tune of $769 for dinner. How palatable would the message of salvation be to those who need it if they believed the church genuinely cared for their needs in a practical way?

Your homework assignment is to read Genesis chapters 13 & 14 before continuing.

Genesis 14:19-24 (NLT)
[19] Melchizedek blessed Abram with this blessing:
"Blessed be Abram by God Most High, Creator of heaven and earth.
[20] And blessed be God Most High, who has defeated your enemies for you."
Then Abram gave Melchizedek a tenth of all the goods he had recovered.
[21] The king of Sodom said to Abram, "Give back my people who were captured. But you may keep for yourself all the goods you have recovered."
[22] Abram replied to the king of Sodom, "I solemnly swear to the LORD, God Most High, Creator of heaven and earth,
[23] that I will not take so much as a single thread or sandal thong from what belongs to you. Otherwise you might say, 'I am the one who made Abram rich.'
[24] I will accept only what my young warriors have already eaten, and I request that you give a fair share of the goods to my allies— Aner, Eshcol, and Mamre."

We have been told that it takes money to spread the gospel. I don't know where this started, but it is this kind of thinking that keeps us from demonstrating the simplicity of Christianity. It costs you nothing to tell someone your testimony and to tell them about Jesus. Tell them that Jesus loves them and has a better life awaiting them if they would but accept Him as their Savior. No amount of money in the world could ever replace a kind word spoken in love. Let me remind you because I know you haven't heard this in a while but...

Salvation is free, so go tell it on the mountain, over the hills and everywhere. Just give it away. Freely you have received, freely give.

CHAPTER 10

13: The Number of Rebellion Against Oppressive Authorities

The number 13 represents rebellion against oppressive leaders and this number shows up for the first time in the 14th chapter of the book of Genesis. Now let us talk about the heart of the matter. I want you to look at the hearts of two men. After Abraham returned with his nephew Lot and the recovered possessions, the King of Sodom said to Abraham "keep the loot, just give the people back to me". The heart that the King of Sodom had for the people he led is often misunderstood. Bera who was the king of Sodom wanted his people to be free from the oppressive leadership of Chedorlaomer who was the king of Elam, so he and a few of his friends who had finally had enough rebelled. Their rebellion did not come without a price though. You see Bera had risked his life by speaking out against and challenging those oppressive leaders. He took them on and lost miserably.

If Chedorlaomer had left Lot alone, Abraham would never have been drawn into the battle. A lesson to every oppressive leader is to never abuse someone who is loved. You may oppress them but you have to remember that they are not alone. Abraham killed the oppressor and those who were in allegiance to him. The second lesson is to those who support oppressive leaders either through their silence or via open support. Judgment is sure, complete and all-encompassing to the entire corrupt system of oppression.

When Abraham returned from slaughtering these oppressive kings, Bera was so appreciative that his people were finally free that he said to Abraham, keep the stuff because all I ever really cared about were the people. Abraham considered the offer being made to him. Because he was motivated by love, he refused the money settling only for the return of his nephew Lot. Keeping the money was a good idea, but it was not a God idea. It never is. Let me explain. Abraham did something for Bera that Bera and his oppressed friends could not do for themselves. He defeated an oppressive enemy who was stronger than them. Their rebellion sparked the fight that would ultimately lead to their deliverance. They had finally grown tired of talking about the problems in the kingdom and decided to do something about them. What's interesting is that it was the enemy's actions against Abraham's nephew Lot that drew Abraham into the fight. Had it not been for the rebellion of the good leaders against the oppressive ones, five kingdoms of people would have continued to live under the oppressive dictatorship of an unjust ruler. In the same way that Abraham brought deliverance to Lot by defeating the oppressive king named Chedorlaomer and his friends, Christ defeated the oppressive king of darkness called Satan and delivered you and I from his control and the control of those who serve him.

Had Chedorlaomer left Lot alone, he would have never faced a man motivated by love. Chedorlaomer was used to bullying people around unchallenged, but the stage was set and the time came when he simply picked on the wrong man. I want you to know that Abraham was to Lot, who Jesus Christ is to you and

I. The enemy has launched a full debilitating assault against you and you feel helpless to defend yourself against much of what has happened to you. Do not fear because God has been watching it all, the time is now and Christ has come in your defense.

After careful consideration of the offer being made to him Abraham simply stated, "No thank you to the money, I'll just take my nephew whom I love." Have you ever heard your pastor utter these words: "Thank you for your money, but no thank you; it is not about the money, it is about you." I think this is a wonderful example of a man who had a healthy perspective regarding money and ministry.

CHAPTER 11

The Changing Face of Christianity

A simple blood test would reveal Abraham as the father of two great nations of people, Jews and Arabs. Christianity is derived from the Jews. The Islamic or Muslim faith is derived from the Arabs. An astounding 53 percent of the world's population is monotheistic, being Jewish, Christian, or Muslim. Christianity currently represents the largest group of monotheistic religious believers in the world.

Based on present growth rates for the world population and religious groups, in roughly 180 years, half of the world's population will be Muslim. If the growth rate continues as it currently is, in eighty years Islam will surpass Christianity and become the world's largest faith-based group. Islam's rapid growth is mostly the result of a higher birth rate among its followers, but Islam also wins more than it loses through conversions. In other words, they are winning souls and they are out winning us. A task that is not hard to believe considering we have left off from witnessing and soul winning. If you are reading this book and you are a Christian, write today's date on the first line. On the second line write down the number of people you have talked to one on one about salvation in the past twelve months. On the third line record the number of souls you have won to Christ in the last twelve months.

_____

Today's date

_____

_____

If you are too embarrassed to log your figures now, I want you to write today's date below and come back to this chapter twelve months from now and record your updated totals on the lines below. Set a calendar reminder so that you do not forget and go after souls for the Kingdom of God.

_____

One year from previously recorded date

_____

_____

It would appear that the message of soul-saving salvation has lost its luster to the more palatable preaching of prosperity. Testing the elasticity of Christianity, we have created one-way dialogues in our congregations by taking (un**profit**able) Sunday school out of the church. The trend for midweek services resembles Sunday morning's spoon-fed approach to a lecture about God's word. Because of the declining two way dialogue about the Word of God, ignorance is growing at an alarming rate throughout Christianity. Most struggle to articulate the difference between sin vs. sins; reconciliation vs. redemption; law vs. grace. You would be surprised to know how many do not know the story of David and Goliath, Gideon's Army or the three Hebrew boys in the fiery furnace. These are basic Sunday school lessons. The worn tracks of the old path are fading fast as its grounds are grown over for the lack of use by the curious traveler. Like the nine-month bulge in the belly of a pregnant woman, we too are about to give birth to a new offspring of Christian believers, but the coming generation bears no resemblance to the Father.

If we continue going in our current direction, one has to wonder, will anyone actually be saved when Christ returns to redeem the church He has given His life for? **We complained about prayer being taken out of our schools, but I am concerned that we have taken the gospel out of our preaching.**

When I look into the face of today's Christianity, I do not recognize her. She has changed a whole lot. Being about my Father's business is slowly taking on a whole new meaning as we only hire family or those with degrees (never mind being anointed and called by God). The subtle preaching of humanism appears to be taking precedence over simple yet genuine gospel preaching. "God is going to give you a strategy for that business plan. Just sow for where you want to go" is what you are told. To the untrained ear, this sounds Godly, but to those who are mature in the word, they understand that these words are spoken in error. What is not so obvious is the manipulation used by the minister to take advantage of those who are ambitious and frustrated with the progress of their lives. Many are looking for answers to help them advance in their endeavors but are left only to find empty promises that mirror their empty bank accounts.

Jesus is the answer for the world today; above him there is no other. Money is not, nor will it ever be the answer to your problems. Plainly stated, stop chasing wealth. It will not solve your problems. Here is a simple five-step formula to help eliminate your money woes. You will only be successful with the implementation of these steps if you eliminate those things in your life that demand what little money you have.

Christian Chart 1a

Muslim Chart 2b

1. Don't need *anything*. Be content.
2. Don't live above and beyond the money you currently have.
3. If you can't afford it, don't buy it. This includes worship facilities, television broadcasts, vehicles, clothes, and the latest electronics.
4. Don't live on credit. You will inevitably pay more for the things you buy.
5. Don't let anyone talk you out of your money.

In order to eliminate the discontentment that plagues us, we must rid ourselves of its source: the need for things. Many are walking away from their marriages, abandoning lifelong relationships, and cutting off loved ones because they are dissatisfied, discontent, and unfulfilled. The root cause to why so many are throwing in the towel on what should be lifelong commitments is a change in their expectations. Let me explain. Many couples who have been married for years leave their spouses and fall completely out of love, because they feel that they should be a lot farther in life than they are. They believe that somehow their spouse is holding them back. If I can get rid of you, I can be farther because I can do bad all by myself is how they reason. The preacher comes along and reinforces this destructive thinking by telling them, they will have to tell some people goodbye and cut them off. Walk away is what they are told. All this is done in the name of getting ahead. This is foolishness! Stay with your spouse and whatever you have or do not have, you will have or not have it together. The only needs you should have in life are God, family, food and shelter. The rest you really can do without.

Faith in its simplest definition is believing you have received something even-though you cannot see it or have not yet received it. Faith is the act of believing. Your faith is built or developed on the basis of what you hear. Preaching is designed to build your faith. What you hear should be rooted in the word of God. If you change what you are hearing, you change what your faith is rooted in. Sunday mornings are filled with sermons that focus on success and wealth in *this* life. These messages have successfully begun shifting the believers expectations to a worldly focus.

Jeremiah 23:1-2 (NLT)
"What sorrow awaits the leaders of my people—the shepherds of my sheep—for they have destroyed and scattered the very ones they were expected to care for," says the LORD.
2 Therefore, this is what the LORD, the God of Israel, says to these shepherds: "Instead of caring for my flock and leading them to safety, you have deserted them and driven them to destruction. Now I will pour out judgment on you for the evil you have done to them.

Today's preaching is nothing like the preaching of our childhood. If you change the preaching, the faith will inevitably follow. Simply stated, we have changed the foundation of what our faith is built upon because pastors have changed what is being preached. I have written a poem that I believe better illustrates this point.

I BELIEVE
Hearing fosters believing,
Believing produces behavior.
If you want to know what I will do,
Listen to what I believe.
If you want to know what I believe,
Take a look at what I do.
I do not believe everything I hear,
But everything I do
Is rooted in what I heard,
I believe.

The foundation of doing is believing. People do what they believe. The root to believing is hearing. You can influence a person's belief by controlling their source of information. Whoever controls the source of information possesses the power to influence behavioral trends.

Frustration has settled in all across Christianity as many struggle to reconcile the difference between their beliefs (what they are being told over the pulpit) and their realities. The catastrophic result is that many have left off from focusing on building their hopes on things eternal and are not preparing themselves for success in the next life.

Looking Glass – Easily Broken?

"I just don't feel like our marriage is going anywhere," she says. Angrily he replies, "How can you say that to me after all I have put up with from you, your mother, and your *^&!$#@% girlfriends?" His voice is raised. His shoulders are visibly tense as he grasps the steering wheel with a white-knuckle grip. His head leans forward ever so slightly as he stares straight ahead. Rain beats fiercely on the windshield as he struggles to control his emotions and see the road in front of him. The sun roof is leaking, but no one seems to notice. "Squeak, squeak, squeak, squeak" the wiper blades rapidly swipe back and forth across the windshield. It is difficult to see what's ahead. Emotionally fueled, unconsciously he is accelerating. In addition to losing his job, he is fed up with the constant threats of divorce and being reminded of how he is not "man enough." The thought of violently crashing the SUV into a tree crosses his mind. He thinks about the life insurance policy that will go to his children so he knows they will be alright if they survive the crash. Besides they are sitting in the back seat, buckled up. Suddenly a minister comes across the radio in the background, "The Bible says, Husbands, love your wives as Christ has loved the church." He does not know why, but this has captured his attention. He tunes out the barrage of heated chatter coming from the passenger seat from the woman who once said she loved him.

She fires back, "Do not bring my mother into this; if it wasn't for her, we would be living on the streets. I didn't see anyone from your uppity family trying to help us when we needed it. Besides any real man would find a way to provide the things his wife needs. You never buy me things and we never go to the places that I like. All my friends went to the Grammy's this past weekend. Do you know how it feels not to be able to go to something as important that? Man I tell you my friends were right, you really are a looser."

Cringed together in the backseat with visible signs of matrimonial stress on their faces, Lottie, Shinab, Shemeber, and Zoar, their four children, brace themselves as the fiery tongue-lashings start again. Neither Mom nor Dad notices these four witnesses, who have had a front-row seat for the past seven years in how to be successful in building a toxic relationship. Shinab, the second older and more aware child begins to hyperventilate as he rocks back and forth clenching his ears. His younger brother Zoar tries to console him. The older boy has not yet learned how to cope with the stress of it all.

This silent majority has already cast their votes on who is right and who is wrong. But they are torn because they love mommy and daddy alike. The older sister Lottie is frozen as her eyes are fixed on the heated argument taking place in the front seat. Accustomed to the emotionally charged atmosphere, Lottie who is just like her mother has grown immune to its effects. Her eyes are fixed on the front passenger seat as she studies every word that proceeds out of her mother's mouth.

The young wife wants to fulfill her life ambitions but believes she has gone as far in life as she can go with her husband. She is told, "You cannot take everybody with you into this next move of God. You will have to walk away from some people and tell them good-bye." Suddenly discontentment begins to take root in the heart of the one who hears these words. She believes she cannot get "there" with him. This nameless wife is symbolic of those who believe they are in a relationship with an individual who is not going anywhere and who cannot help them get to the next level in life. It will not be long before her belief manifests itself into action. Her actions are fueled by what she believes. What she believes is rooted in the modern day message being preached over the pulpit at the family's local church.

Without the preaching of the gospel, how can anyone be saved?

> *Romans 10:13-17*
> *[13] For whosoever shall call upon the name of the Lord shall be saved.*
> *[14] How then shall they call on him in whom they have not believed? and how shall they believe in him of whom they have not heard? and how shall they hear without a preacher?*
> *[15] And how shall they preach, except they be sent? as it is written, How beautiful are the feet of them that preach the gospel of peace, and bring glad tidings of good things!*
> *[16] But they have not all obeyed the gospel. For Esaias saith, Lord, who hath believed our report?*
> *[17] So then faith cometh by hearing, and hearing by the word of God.*

I have no doubt that we will be having church in thirty years, but by what standard? The standards I see being raised today look nothing like the standard of truth from the church of my early childhood. I am deeply concerned. We have strayed from the path. Thirty years from now scares me as I assess what kinds of Christians we will be. Will anyone living at that time actually be preaching the "go tell it on the mountain" message of redemption? We are not in need of a revival in our churches; we are in desperate need of a funeral. The call goes out to bury many of the practices which have a purely business focus in our churches today. Pastors, we are crying out for a change. Are there any fathers still alive in our churches that have the Godly nerve to clear their throats and set the house in order? I pray to God that these kinds of seasoned men and women of God have not all died off before passing on their wisdom and experience of holiness.

Sunday after Sunday we are held hostage by a new breed of Christian leaders who have an insatiable appetite for the lion's share of prosperity, prestige, position, power, and control. We do not need a revival we need a resurrection! Buried under the onslaught of things this world has to offer, the missing ingredients are good old-fashioned contentment coupled with Bible based preaching! We have to seek the old paths once walked by those who knew less theology but lived more Bible. My heart aches for the days when the focus of Christianity was clear, non-complicated and non-competitive; a time when the preacher and the congregants were truly after souls not worldly possessions. I long for the time when the norm was quality community churches that focused on loving families and their neighborhoods. Today that focus appears to be on programs, status and brands.

1 John 2:15-17
[15] Love not the world, neither the things that are in the world. If any man love the world, the love of the Father is not in him.
[16] For all that is in the world, the lust of the flesh, and the lust of the eyes, and the pride of life, is not of the Father, but is of the world.
[17] And the world passeth away, and the lust thereof: but he that doeth the will of God abideth for ever.

My uncle, whose opinion I respect greatly, once told me to always keep in mind that "You cannot address the mess if you are a part of the mess." I will never forget it as long as I live. I believe that Compromise causes you to alter your plans, resulting in a change in your goals, rendering you ineffective in your achievements.

Matthew 5:13 (NLT)
"You are the salt of the earth. But what good is salt if it has lost its flavor? Can you make it salty again? It will be thrown out and trampled underfoot as worthless.

The world has lost respect for what the church has to offer due to growing compromise within. Because of the communal embrace of compromise within the ranks of Christian leadership, we have shifted our focus from that which was given to us in the Great Commission.

Mark 16: 15-20 (NLT)
[15]And then he told them, "Go into all the world and preach the Good News to everyone, everywhere.
[16]Anyone who believes and is baptized will be saved. But anyone who refuses to believe will be condemned.
[17]These signs will accompany those who believe: They will cast out demons in my name, and they will speak new languages.
[18]They will be able to handle snakes with safety, and if they drink anything poisonous, it won't hurt them. They will be able to place their hands on the sick and heal them."
[19]When the Lord Jesus had finished talking with them, he was taken up into heaven and sat down in the place of honor at God's right hand.
[20]And the disciples went everywhere and preached, and the Lord worked with them, confirming what they said by many miraculous signs.

Luke 24:47
With my authority, take this message of repentance to all the nations, beginning in Jerusalem: 'There is forgiveness of sins for all who turn to me.'

2 Corinthians 5:18-20
[18] And all of this is a gift from God, who brought us back to himself through Christ. And God has given us this task of reconciling people to him.
[19] For God was in Christ, reconciling the world to himself, no longer counting people's sins against them. And he gave us this wonderful message of reconciliation.
[20] So we are Christ's ambassadors; God is making his appeal through us. We speak for Christ when we plead, "Come back to God!"
[21] For God made Christ, who never sinned, to be the offering for our sin, so that we could be made right with God through Christ.

CHAPTER 12

My Sheep Know My Voice

I have a little exercise I want you to participate in. You should spend no more than 30 minutes per day for three days to complete the entire exercise. Complete this exercise even if you are already a born-again professing Christian believer.

I call it "My Sheep Know My Voice."

Repeat this exercise once per day over the next three calendar days and record your activity.

Day 1 _____/_____/_____
INTERACTION WITH CHRISTIAN MEDIA

Step 1:
Turn your television, radio, Smartphone, or YouTube to any Christian station and listen for a total of 15 to 20 minutes to any sermon.

Step 2:
Using the "My Father's Voice Litmus Test" below answer the questions.

Question #1:
What insights did you gain from this exercise?

_____

_____

Question #2:
Did the message or interaction focus on Christ?

_____

_____

Question #3:
Were you compelled to give money or your life at the end of the sermon?

_____

_____

Question #4: Was the message relevant?

_____

_____

Question #5:

Were you offered the opportunity to come to know Christ? Did you accept Him as your savior? If yes call someone and tell him/her the good news. If no, what specifically is preventing you from doing so?

_____

_____

Question #6:

What changes are you prepared to make in your personal handling of God's word based on what you have just heard?

_____

_____

Question #7:

When will you implement these changes? Circle one: Immediately | Sometime in the future | I'm not prepared to implement any changes at this time.

Day 2 _____/_____/_____
INTERACTION WITH A PROFESSING CHRISTIAN

Step 1:
Start a general conversation with any Christian believer who is not a pastor, deacon, elder or bishop (this includes their spouses as well) regarding what they believe you are called to do in life.

Step 2:
Answer the questions below using the "My Father's Voice Litmus Test".

Question #1:
How do I find my calling in life?

_____

_____

Question #2:
Did his/her answer or the interaction focus on Christ?

_____

_____

Question #3:
Were you compelled to want to know Christ more?

_____

_____

Question #4:
Was the calling realistic?

_____

_____

Question #5:
Did he/she offer you the opportunity to come to know Christ?
Did you accept Him as your savior? If yes call someone and
tell him/her the good news. If no, what specifically is pre-
venting you from doing so?

_____

_____

Question #6:
What changes are you prepared to make in your life based on
your interaction with the Christian you just spoke with?

_____

_____

Question #7:
When will you implement these changes? Circle one:
Immediately | Sometime in the future | I'm not prepared to
implement any changes at this time.

_____

_____

Day 3 _____/_____/_____
INTERACTION WITH CHRISTIAN LEADERSHIP

Step 1:
Even if you are already a professing Christian, I want you to start a general conversation with a Christian leader regarding your calling in life. This doesn't have to be someone you know. They must be a pastor, elder, minister, deacon, etc. This can include the leader's spouse. ***If you are a leader, speak with someone who does not know you are a leader in the Christian community***

Step 2:
Using the "My Father's Voice Litmus Test" below answer the questions.

Question #1:
How do I find my calling in life?

_____

_____

Question #2:
Did the calling or interaction focus on Christ?

_____

_____

Question #3:
Were you compelled to want to know Christ better?

_____

_____

Question #4:
Was the counsel they provided clear or confusing?

_____

_____

Question #5:
Did the leader offer you the opportunity to come to know Christ? Did you accept him as your savior? If yes call someone and tell him/her the good news. If no, what specifically is preventing you from doing so?

_____

_____

Question #6:
What changes are you prepared to make in your life based on your interaction with the Christian Leader you just spoke with?

_____

_____

Question #7:
When will you implement these changes? Circle One: Immediately | Sometime in the future | I'm not prepared to implement any changes at this time.

_____

_____

At the end of the three day exercise, I want you to evaluate your findings.

Instructions:

Evaluate the last three days and list the similarities and differences for the answers you received for each consecutive question. Compare question one for day one with question one for days two and three. Do this for each question for all three days until you have completed all the correlated questions.

Question #1

_____

_____

Question #2

_____

_____

Question #3

_____

_____

Question #4

_____

_____

Question #5

_____

_____

Question #6

_____

_____

Question #7

_____

_____

Now that you have completed this three-day exercise, your final step is to share your experience with others. I realize this may be a challenge for many of you. I am asking you to begin sharing your experience because I believe we have to urgently be about the Father's business of spreading the news of Christ to everyone. WE NEED URGENCY IN CHRISTIANITY WITH WITNESSING AND WINNING SOULS TO CHRIST, WE HAVE GOTTEN LAZY. We have to get this generations blood off our hands! EVERYONE you talk to, you should be asking yourself, "Does this person know Jesus?"

Push yourself! I believe you can do it.
You're stronger than what you think you are.

The purpose of this exercise is twofold. I wanted you to gain new insights regarding how we are sharing our experience in Christ with others. From these insights you should begin to see how important it is that we are all on the same page when it comes to pointing people to Him. Secondly I believe God wants to ignite a fire in you to be-gin randomly sharing your Christian experience with others so you can begin the process of leading them to Christ. You can do it. You should do it. You are commanded to do it. The more you do it, the easier it becomes to share your Christian experience with others.

II Corinthians 5:19-20 (NLT)
[17] This means that anyone who belongs to Christ has become a new person. The old life is gone; a new life has begun!
[18] And all of this is a gift from God, who brought us back to him-self through Christ. And God has given us this task of reconciling people to him.
[19] For God was in Christ, reconciling the world to himself, no longer counting people's sins against them. And he gave us this wonderful message of reconciliation.
[20] So we are Christ's ambassadors; God is making his appeal through us. We speak for Christ when we plead, "Come back to God!"
[21] For God made Christ, who never sinned, to be the offering for our sin, so that we could be made right with God through Christ.

CHAPTER 13

Almighty Dollar – Money, Money, Money...Money!

G od does not mind you having money. God minds money having you. Many leaders open themselves up to all kinds of unnecessary problems because they have fallen in love with money.

1 Timothy 6:6-14 (NLT)
⁶Yet true godliness with contentment is itself great wealth.
⁷After all, we brought nothing with us when we came into the world, and we can't take anything with us when we leave it.
⁸So if we have enough food and clothing, let us be content.
⁹But people who long to be rich fall into temptation and are trapped by many foolish and harmful desires that plunge them into ruin and destruction.
¹⁰For the love of money is the root of all kinds of evil. And some people, craving money, have wandered from the true faith and pierced themselves with many sorrows.

The next few verses are the apostle Paul's instructions to a young preacher whom he has been mentoring and preparing for ministry.

I Timothy 6:11-14 (NLT)
*[11]But you, Timothy, are a man of God; so run from all these evil
things. Pursue righteousness and a godly life, along with faith,
love, perseverance, and gentleness*
*[12]Fight the good fight for the true faith. Hold tightly to the eternal
life to which God has called you, which you have confessed so
well before many witnesses*
*[13]And I charge you before God, who gives life to all, and before
Christ Jesus, who gave a good testimony before Pontius Pilate,*
*[14]that you obey this command without wavering. Then no one
can find fault with you from now until our Lord Jesus Christ
comes again.*

**I once overheard my father tell one of my brothers,
"Enough money can change anyone."**

With a warm and gentle voice hugged with the honey of
life, my wife always says, "Having more money only makes you
more of who you really are."

There are unlimited negative effects that greed and the need
for money can have on people and the things they are willing to
do to get more of it. In the book of 1st Timothy, the apostle Paul
mentors Timothy, who is a young up-and-coming preacher. He
warns him about the dangers of having the wrong focus regarding ministry and money. It would appear that our leaders have
begun preaching a message that engenders a lack of contentment
within the hearts of today's believers. Frustrated with not seeing
our dreams become realities, we now insist on having the things
we hope for. As a result we are no longer satisfied with what we
have, and having God alone is simply not enough.

Shhh, if you listen closely, you can hear it all over the airways:
"God wants you to be rich." "This is your year." "Riches, wealth,
and money come to me now!" "I will not be broke another day in my

life." "God has a seven-step financial plan to make you wealthy." "Sow a seed of one thousand dollars, and watch God release a harvest in your life." "If you want the blessings I spoke of to come into your life, get a financial seed in your hand. You have to respond to God with an offering." "Sow for where you want to go." "It takes a seed to meet your need." "It's God's will for you to be a millionaire, I see millionaires all in this room. Go ahead and get a seed in your hands and sow one thousand dollars towards your millions, halleluiah to God." The pursuit of happiness has bogarted its way into the hearts of many of God's people and now sits brazenly on the throne of their lives. Guard your heart child of God.

The Bible says more about money than it does about the blood of Jesus. I want to list several scriptures to guide you in your walk. Unless otherwise indicated, each verse is taken from the New Living Translation.

1. *1 Timothy 6:10 For the love of money is the root of all kinds of evil. And some people, craving money, have wandered from the true faith and pierced themselves with many sorrows.*

2. *Hebrews 13:5 Don't love money; be satisfied with what you have. For God has said, "I will never fail you. I will never abandon you."*

3. *1 Timothy 3:3 He must not be a heavy drinker or be violent. He must be gentle, not quarrelsome, **and not love money**.*

4. *Luke 16:14 The Pharisees, who dearly loved their money, heard all this and scoffed at him.*

5. *Ecclesiastes 5:10 **Those who love money will never have enough.** How meaningless to think that wealth brings true happiness!*

6. *Matthew 6:24 No one can serve two masters. For you will hate one and love the other; you will be devoted to one and despise the other. **You can not serve both God and money.***

7. *2 Timothy 3:2 (ESV) For people will be lovers of self, **lovers of money,** proud, arrogant, abusive, disobedient to their parents, ungrateful, unholy,*

8. *1 Samuel 8:3 But they were not like their father, for* **they were greedy for money.** *They accepted bribes and perverted justice.*

9. *Psalm 119:36 Give me an eagerness for your laws rather than* **a love for money!**

10. *2 Corinthians 12:15* **I will gladly spend myself and all I have for you,** *even though it seems that the more I love you, the less you love me.*

11. *1 John 3:17 If someone has enough money to live well and sees a brother or sister in need but shows no compassion—how can God's love be in that person?*

12. *John 12:4-6 ⁴But Judas Iscariot, the disciple who would soon betray him, said, ⁵That perfume was worth a year's wages. It should have been sold and the money given to the poor." ⁶Not that he cared for the poor—* **he was a thief, and since he was in charge of the disciples' money, he often stole some for himself.**

13. *Mark 10:21 Looking at the man, Jesus felt genuine love for him. "There is still one thing you haven't done," he told him. "Go and sell all your possessions and* **give the money to the poor, and you will have treasure in heaven.** *Then come, follow me."*

14. *Ezekiel 33:3 So my people come pretending to be sincere and sit before you. They listen to your words, but they have no intention of doing what you say. Their mouths are full of lustful words, and* **their hearts seek only after money.**

15. *2 Peter 2:15 They have wandered off the right road and followed the footsteps of Balaam son of Beor,* **who loved to earn money by doing wrong.**

My spirit is troubled that with each passing year the message of the cross, which saves souls, is becoming less and less of a priority as we see the Christian conversion rate rapidly declining. We have lost our focus for witnessing and replaced it with marketing. I believe with all my heart that fliers, commercials, and Internet streams are less effective than one-on-one conversations. It is old fashioned but sharing your personal testimony with a nonbeliever face-to-face cannot be beat. Offering him/her the chance to come to know Christ for him/herself and see that look on their face is priceless when they do. I'm not suggesting that we should not do those other things, but I am saying that we should not abandon our responsibility to talk to people about Christ. No flyer can ever compete with human emotion and good ole eye-to-eye contact.

Our church buildings are getting bigger, opulently outfitted with more expensive, sophisticated smart technology. The message of salvation is increasingly being drowned out by messages designed to sell CDs. Our growth appears to be a false positive as we have filled our pews with recycled Christians from the other shepherds' fold. One visit to another church down the street and you will quickly find out what happened to that family we used to see on Sundays. We simply fill their spots with the family who came from the church you visited down the street. We are not growing, because we have stopped talking to sinners about Christ.

New converts are falling through the cracks at an alarming rate, as we place little to no efforts on a robust, follow-up initiative after they have accepted Christ as Lord and Savior. Here is a foolproof system to help you hold on to newly converted believers, it is called relationships. New believers are finding it difficult to live empowered lives after feeding on today's motivational messages designed to prepare them for the next blessing but not for the next life. Churches are huge, but the internal relationships are clogged at the top and do not filter down into everyday practical life. "I'll see you next Sunday" defines the depth of our relationships with one another. "I love you sister" goes no farther than the pew that you share, and "I got your back brother" never materializes into the lending of that back to help you move a heavy refrigerator. Fictitious, empty, void and phony; relationships today have no more weight or substance than a bowl of cotton candy. They are fluffy and sweet but void of real life-giving nourishment.

I grew up in a predominantly matriarchal family. My mom and aunties are southern girls, so they made it a point to get all the children together every single weekend for family time. Cards (spades of course); barbeques, music, hide-n-seek for the kids' man we had lots of fun just playing in the middle of the street. There was often a lot of cussin, yes cussin! More importantly we built real relationships. They were weighted down and anchored in an unbreakable love that my cousins and entire family still have for one another to this day. We are Garner Blood Garner Strong!

How do we fix the lack of real genuine brotherly love that is so desperately needed in the church and the world today? It begins with shifting our focus from the need for money and all the things that it can buy us, to focusing on truly loving people. I mean loving them to the extent that you find it nearly impossible to live without them. Yes, I mean putting up with them and all their crazy ways but telling them the truth about themselves. Telling them how you feel to their face (in love) even if it leads to an argument; just don't talk about them behind their backs because that is more hurtful. Don't be afraid to have the food fight! The food fight begins with seniors correcting young people who do things that you know are not good for them and making them respect you. Share your wisdom and when needed do not bite your tongue. What are you afraid of? You are three times older than they are! It begins with obeying that voice within you that tells you to be kind. They are probably going to burn you but open your home to that struggling couple and help them out. You will not miss whatever you give to them. I know you have given your sister money before and she has not paid you back from the first time. Loan you sister the money again if she really needs it and forget about it. You will make more money, besides you will blow more on junk than you loan to her anyway. Check on your neighbor to make sure she is alright and stop walking past people like you do not see them. Smile and speak to strangers at the supermarket. Be courageous enough to tell your husband that he cannot trust the intentions of every woman who is not you. It may help you avoid divorce. Discipline your children without apology but do not abuse them because it teaches them to abuse others later in life. I know your teenager has a funky attitude but so what, you are not permitted to give up on her, she is your daughter. If she slams the door you open it and tell her "not in my house." She will thank you for it later in life. Do not argue without apologizing. I don't see any angels down here living this life, it's just us. Do not hold on to hurts because in the end they only hurt you. Remember the whole world knows that the only perfect man to ever have lived is Jesus, so forgive people when they do wrong because you recognize that you yourself are not perfect.

I know you have been told to walk away and cut people loose, but I am saying that the most important investments you will ever make in life are not the ones that you tuck away in an envelope and wave before God on Sunday mornings. Your greatest investments in life will always be the ones you make in people. This is how we fix the mess that we have gotten ourselves into.

You should really get to know the people God has brought into your life. Do you remember when life used to be like this and Church used to reinforce these kinds of behaviors? Do not let anyone tell you that you may have to cut people loose. As you get back into reading your bible, you will find that Jesus teaches a very different philosophy. The teaching that encourages you to walk away from anyone who is "holding you back" is perpetuated by those who have a focus on prosperity, promotion and getting ahead by any means necessary. Do not follow down that crooked path.

I want to encourage you to break free from being the kind of Christian, whose only encounter with the people and the word of God is what you experience on Sunday mornings. Here are some ways you can begin engrafting the word of God into you daily life: Fry some fish and invite some people over to help you eat it. Don't forget to invite your neighbors. Invite four people to your home after Sunday morning service to watch the game or a movie. Make two dozen sliders along with some chips and your favorite beverages. Find one passage of scripture each week, such as the *23rd Psalm* or *2 Corinthians 5:19-20*. Memorize it by reading it first thing in the morning and let it be the last thing you read at night. Quote them periodically to yourself throughout the day over the course of the week. I want you to develop and nurture a sincere hunger for the things that God is passionate about. Start a club for memorizing and quoting scriptures!

We have to guard our hearts against becoming selfish in our pursuit for the things of God? I can remember a time in the middle of a powerful, soul-saving sermon when people would come to the front of the church broken, with tears streaming down their faces, and lay their lives on the altar. Now they come in the middle of the sermon with a smile on their faces and lay their money on the altar instead! This is foolishness, I wish I knew of another way to describe it, but nothing else quite fits.

We have to shift our focus to those things that truly matter. There was a time when every sermon ended with an altar call, followed by two and sometimes three compelling pleas urging sinners that

"Tomorrow is not promised to you. If you died tonight, where would you spend eternity? Give your life to Christ before it is too late".

When sinners came, we took as much time as was needed to help them lay their burdens down. Disturbingly we are seeing more and more of a trend in which the sermon ends with a strong appeal, instructing the people to give more money to Christ and pick up the CD on your way out so I can tell you again what the Bible says. Very little emphasis is placed on studying the word for yourself. The sermons end with a "stick 'em up" appeal as the speaker parades an array of products before you, strongly urging you to "stop by my table." I wish I could fully express the heaviness I feel in my spirit concerning this. I'm disturbed that there is even a need to address such foolery. My heart is truly broken over the direction in which I see our fathers taking church today. Every time I see another brother or sister launch "xyz Ministries" my heart sinks. Why do so many feel the need to put their names on God's business? I see them set off to walk a path that is often broad and filled with crooked roads of uncertainty, and many seem to find it.

Jesus expressed his dissatisfaction with this kind of approach to ministry when he kicked over the tables of the money changers in the temple. He was not being disrespectful to the presence of God. He understood that God had left that place a long time ago, and someone had to arrest that generation of insensitive leaders. He also knew that one week later they would crucify him for his actions.

Do you remember Jesus's indictment against the leaders? He accused them of turning the house of prayer into a den of thieves who had shifted their focus from prayer to one where they peddled their products to the people. Books, music CDs, T-shirts, DVDs, water bottles, caps, and license plate covers...all in the name of a God who never sees the proceeds.

CHAPTER 14

Return to Sender

M alachi is not your letter; it belongs to your leader. It is
a letter written to every leader who has ill-gotten gains
through means of purposeful manipulation. They freely fleece
the innocent and leave God what they cannot use for themselves. Their conscience is silenced by their insatiable appetites
for more. They are like the sea that drinks in water, they are
never satisfied.

I want to share a story with you about two men who dared
to challenge the system. Like David against Goliath and Elijah
against Jazebel's system of control; these two men would face
formidable adversaries in the form of religious leaders who were
not ready to relinquish the strong hold they had on the minds
and hearts of the people. These leaders had a marketing system/
scheme they used that brought them an enormous amount of
wealth. It was marketing at its best! Innocently enough they used
a young girl who could foretell the future. She would provide insights into future events for anyone who wanted to know what the
future held for them, and the leaders would charge a fee for her
insights. That's right they were charging people to receive a word.

The problem with this is that she was using her abilities to uphold a system that took advantage of God's people and brought great wealth to those in charge. We call this ill-gotten gain.

Ask anyone who is wealthy, and he/she will tell you that having wealth has its own share of unique challenges. The problem here is not with being wealthy. I do not believe it's wrong to be wealthy. I do, however, believe that wealth is best had by those who are mature. For some, wealth brings out the worst in them. The problem rests with how these men obtained their wealth. Anytime you obtain ill-gotten gains you should expect that someone with honest intentions will call you into accountability for it. First they took advantage of a young woman's abilities. She had received a special oratorical gift from God. She possessed one of the speaking gifts. When these men began manipulating her gift for personal profits, her gift became perverted because she was no longer using it for the purpose that it was intended. Secondly, they took advantage of the people who needed what the young woman had to offer. Thirdly, they charged a fee for what was free. They saw an opportunity to make a great deal of money by exploiting the young woman's abilities and charged a hefty fee to anyone who needed what the young woman had to offer.

One day as the two apostles were on their way to prayer, they were met by this young woman who could predict the future. She began following them proclaiming, "These men are the servants of the most high God, which show unto us the way of salvation." (Acts 16:17 KJV) At first the two men simply ignored her. Again she would meet them and follow them around town, proclaiming, "These men are the servants of the most high God..." This went on for several days. The apostles were beginning to realize that some things simply cannot be ignored. The young woman had become so accustomed to having her gift exploited that, she never considered what she was doing could be considered as wrong. Her leaders had used her for so long that she could no longer discern the difference between what was right and what was wrong. She was using her gift, but because she did not understand the purpose it was to serve, she innocently allowed her leaders to abuse it for money. The atmosphere was tense with expectation as a social revolution was brewing and these two preachers were smack dab in the middle of it all.

My father taught me that abuse is abnormal use. Abuse happens when you use something in a way that it was not intended to be used. What does all this have to do with tithing, you may ask? As you keep reading and the chapters unfold, you will see how leaders have used a system of control and manipulation to exploit multiple tax free millions out of the lives of God's people. I said millions because some of you may have a hard time believing that the number is more like billions and even trillions of tax free dollars. The government is silent on this issue for some reason, but we know the truth and refuse to be silent any longer. Pastors know tithing is not required, yet they continue to lay this yoke around the necks of God's people. We have participated in years of sacrificial giving but how many people do you know who are millionaires? The facts remain that we do not see any millionaires being produced in the pews.

She was innocent, but the leaders knew better. If given the opportunity, I'm sure she would have defended their actions with statements such as, "my leader deserves to be blessed", "I should give all I have to my leaders considering all the support they give to me", "There's nothing wrong with my leaders being wealthy, it is the least I can do to show my love to them." "How else are they going to run their business, they need money." "They are businessmen and have their own money so why wouldn't they be wealthy." What she did not know was that the same men that she had come to trust would later abuse two innocent men for doing what God had sent them to do. Because her heart was pure, she never challenged or questioned the actions of those who led her because she believed in them. If she was ever going to be free, God would have to do it because she would never go against her leaders. She believed that asking questions of the leadership was the same as being non-submissive. Hers was a life of obedience and submission. What she did not know is that these things made her a target for abuse and oppression.

Although she felt that something wasn't quite right, she told herself "I can't be worried about what they are doing with the money. I just have to do what I know I'm supposed to do." She turned the whole thing over to God because she simply wanted her gift to be used. She never questioned the method by which the leaders got the money or what they did with it. She thought to herself that as long as she did her part, what they did with the money was between them and God. Well God was about to speak up and express is disapproval of their system. God saw her heart and sent a healthy leader to set his daughter free from the manipulation that she had begun to justify. Just as God sent the apostle Paul to set this innocent woman free from the cunning sleight of those men, in like manner God the father sent this book to free you in your mind and spirit to serve him in understanding free of men's systems. If you do not find freedom after reading this book, it will not be because you were not provided the truth, but it will be because you reasoned the truth away. If you have no desire to be free from manipulative leaders, simply stop reading right here. If you continue reading it is an indication that your spirit is truly hungry for the truth, in which case keep reading and praying for understanding of His word while you read.

Finally, after many days of ignoring her repeated attempts to get their attention, the senior of the two men finally had enough and spoke to the root of the problem that plagued the young woman. He spoke to the spirit that was guiding her actions.

Ironically the same spirit that deceived her into believing she was doing the right thing was the same spirit that courted the selfish desires of the leaders who sought to profit from the young woman's gift. I believe the Holy Spirit wanted this story included in this book because He wants to free someone who feels that their gift is being exploited by someone else for profit. Do not be afraid of them. Take a stand for what you know to be right, even if it means confronting those who are unjustly profiting from your gift. Remember, God wants you to be free!

These two men challenged a system that had been widely accepted as being right. Their conviction to upholding a standard that did not include profiting from people through use of ConManLation did not come without a price. The strategy of the manipulating leaders to stop these men was three-fold.

1. They attempted to distract them from their purpose by redirecting their focus. Whenever you go against the grain of a corrupt system you have to remain focused. Expect to be lied on and have your words twisted. Expect to be misunderstood. You can count on public personal attacks designed to discredit you. They do this by bringing up mistakes you made even if they have to reach back twenty years into your past. When the truth you present is irrefutable and the legitimacy confirmable, they will seek to discredit you personally since they cannot deny the truth of your words.

    The enemy's tactic is designed to redirect your passion, causing you to focus on any rumors that get start. By doing so, you become distracted from focusing on God's strategy. Let me share with you that these things come with the territory, and if you are not willing to handle multidirectional controversy, *don't stir the pot*. Controversy always brings attacks, sometimes from places you did not know existed. Get ready because they will come. While I do not believe you should respond to every critic, there are some things you should never ignore. Turn a deaf ear to rumors, true or fabricated, and finish what you started. You should never ignore the truth contained in your heart.

2. **They threatened them with words** through use of public, verbal humiliation. They did this in hopes of garnering support for their own cause and striking fear in the hearts of the men who challenged their cash cow system. They exercised conmanlation. They knew that if they could discredit the character and actions/teachings of these two men, no one would believe them. They understood that *believing* is one of the fundamental building blocks to being set free from any system that governs people's lives. Your challenge is to stay the course and do what God has called you to do even when what you are doing is being threatened by those who refuse to relinquish their system of ill-gotten gains.

3. **They beat them to teach others** who felt the same way. What was this Ivy League, collegiate-level beating designed to teach the onlookers? Going against the system has consequences! You will be marked. Anyone who says "this is wrong" will be labeled as a troublemaker and someone who has not submitted to the dictatorial teachings of the leadership. These leaders are not mature enough to have an open discussion when there are opposing views. They simply resort to control, manipulation and abuse.

They beat them publically and threw them into jail under the charges of teaching something that the leaders did not support. They did not care that the innocent young woman was set free. It is interesting that they did not charge Paul with teaching error nor did they say that Paul had sinned. Their issue was that Paul and Silas taught the people a truth that they themselves were not ready to teach. Paul's actions taught the people that God wants you free from the systems of men. Paul's teachings threatened their profits. They had them beaten and arrested to shut down their teachings. History has taught us that the oppressed are never willingly set free by the oppressor. Remember Genesis chapter 14. I would like to tell you that you will not suffer if you take a stand for what is right, but that simply would not be the truth. You must pick up your cross just as I have and follow Jesus. Planting your feet firmly in your convictions yields immeasurable long-term benefits beyond your wildest dreams. Many of these benefits will unfold and yield dividends well beyond your human expiration date. I'm trying to tell you that when you consider what is to be gained, the beatings (no matter who they come from or what form they come in) are worth it. You may be ostracized for standing for the truth but your children and your children's children will enjoy the freedom that you fought for. They will thank you for obeying God. Don't you bow and don't break, you are standing for a worthy cause.

I write this knowing full well that just as these men came under fire for standing up and saying enough is enough, so will anyone else who dares to show God's children how to become free from dumb gimmicks and manipulative marketing tricks that make the leaders fat with wealth while the people they lead live daily with lack.

Looking Glass – Integrity

Dear Pastor Bill Dollar,

I tried meeting with you several times because you stopped returning my calls. I called the office and was always told that you were busy or in a meeting. So I'm writing you instead. Don't worry, I'm not pregnant! Thank God! A letter from some guy named Malachi was mistakenly given to me by one of your peers, but after thoroughly reading it from start to finish, I realized it was really for you. The accusations raised in it are pretty severe. While I do not believe you would behave in the manner described in the letter, I also know that you are human. The specific examples God lists are pretty compelling... Say it isn't so! Please pay special attention to the immediate call to action required of you in the third chapter verses five through eleven. I apologize that it took so long to get this to you, but I had been wrestling with a spirit of fear for fourteen years, and it kept me from doing a lot of the things I know I should have already done for God. But hallelujah, those days of fear are over. While I respect you highly, you should know that I am not afraid of you. Your message of fearing and obeying God above fearing and obeying man, well I'm walking in it and for the first time in my life I feel truly free. I am no longer afraid to raise my voice and be heard!

Please do not overlook the seriousness of these charges. After reading the letter for myself, I realize that your actions are negatively impacting my ability to be blessed. The curse God originally intended for you has also been passed on to me, because as my leader you represent me. I just want to go on record by saying I did my part by bringing what I was asked to bring to God. I'm not perfect and I did not always pay my tithes as I should have but I have never stolen God's money. I'm sure you can understand how surprised I was when I found out that you did not do your part in giving God what was right. God knows I am not perfect, but sometimes I didn't pay my tithes because I used the money to help someone who was in need. I do not believe God will have as big a problem with that as he does with what He is saying you stole.

Three Sundays ago, I gave one thousand dollars, my sixty-seven-year-old mother gave her rent money, and my sister withdrew $2,263.29 from her bank account (money she used to make sure Grandma had enough medicine each month for her treatments). She even dropped her diamond ring on the altar as an offering! We all gave "a sacrificial offering until it hurt," just as your visiting preacher friend asked. We have faith that God will take care of our needs because truly you can't beat God when it comes to giving. What puzzles us is that we couldn't help but notice the new CL63 AMG Mercedes Benz you drove up in this past Sunday. I know from my personal experiences with you that we both have some shortcomings, but I love you and I still respect you as a godly leader. I mean no harm, but I have to ask, are you using our hard-earned money for your own selfish needs? Are you really robbing God? You don't have to answer me. I remember your month long teaching series where you taught us to honor you and not question the authority of leadership. However, I don't think it's a good idea for you not to answer the letter God asked Malachi to give to you. Anyway I'll leave that decision in your hands.

Don't worry, we are not going to move our membership over this. We really like this church. We have not found a church that we like as much as we like this one; the state-of-the-art children's ministry and all the latest technology here are *awesome*! If the things God spoke of in the letter he wrote to you are true, I may just start giving all my money directly to needy families and claim the money I give on my taxes. Correct me if I'm wrong, but do you think God would frown upon me for doing that? I don't believe He would, but your teaching suggests differently. In fact I believe God would be pleased with this. Anyway, this won't affect our membership, but it will definitely impact how we give.

We will be praying for your strength as you seek God for how best to correct your course.

PS
Everybody knows how you like to address personal things over the pulpit. Please do not preach on me! If you have something to say to me, I think the right thing to do is have a meeting with me and speak to me directly if you can find time in your busy schedule.

Signed,
Your Loving Church Members and Visitors
We are watching you,
XOXO

CHAPTER 15

God vs. Leaders

The book of Malachi was not written directly to laity. They are addressed in the letter because they have some short coming when it came to giving, but they are not the thieves spoken of in the book. Like a letter from a scorned lover, it was written to the religious leaders who were desecrating their office and stealing from God. One of the ways you give to God is by giving to his people. The leaders were supposed to take what the people brought and place it in the storehouse. Whenever the people had a need, they were comforted in knowing they could go to the storehouse and get what they lacked. Their tithes and offerings never made it to the storehouse because they were stolen by the priests. God took notice of this and spoke up. Today, members who are in need are told, "Our church cannot put its name behind meeting your need, even if your need is life threatening." or "We cannot help you because we don't have it." **We just raised the pastor three hundred thousand tax free dollars just for being a pastor another year, but the practical needs of those who are members go unmet.**

The book of Malachi begins by stating that the letter is addressed to Israel. As you read further, you will begin to see God reveal the secrets of a relationship gone wrong. He goes public and reveals to the nation his disapproval of the "behind closed door" actions of his leaders. He reveals to us the root cause behind why, no matter how much they tithed, they were never going to see the open window, poured out blessings He promised. The divine lens becomes more clearly focused as it sharpens its gaze on what God wants revealed to the intended audience. The language sharpens, and the tone toughens as the charges unfold chapter by chapter. A hush falls over the entire nation, and everyone's ears perk up as it is clear that God is not pleased, and someone's integrity is being called on the carpet!

The people understood what it meant to be unfaithful to God. They were far from perfect, but robbery! Well, that one rested at the doorstep of their leaders, and God was about to call the court to order and present his case.

Looking Glass – All Rise, The Honorable Judge Jehovah Jireh Presiding

Many have flown in on their private jets, while others were driven to the proceedings in their Bentleys and custom charter buses with their images wrapped around them. All have their security detail present with them but the bailiff clears the courtroom of anyone who is not a leader or has a vested interest in the case. The people take their seats and fade into the background as spectators. The leaders are placed on center stage to give an account and answer for their management of God's tithes and offerings.

Court is called to order.

"Where are the provisions and why are my people's needs not being met?" asks God. "We don't know what you mean", the leaders reply. "I saw them bringing their tithes so why is this storehouse empty?" asked God. "Nobody's complaining, they all seem to be happy and no one has met with us to discuss any problems. In fact they just keep interrupting us in the middle of our sermons dropping money on the altar. We figured they didn't need the money. We thought that was strange but we just went with it" Answered the leaders. "Yeah, one lady what's her name with the big... hat put $10,000 in my hand right in the middle of the service." Stated another prominent preacher. "I watched as you asked them to give offerings that I did not ask for. WHERE ARE THOSE OFFERINGS? I gave you priests the oversight to make sure the people were taken care of but all I see is fatness in your stomachs and leanness in theirs!" The leaders are all looking around at each other. No one answers for fear of self-incrimination. "Don't make me ask you again. Where is all that you have taken in from these people? And don't tell me that you built a building with it because I never asked you to build me a house, I'm building my own house!" Finally one of the famous premier preachers speaks up and says "We have expenses and most of what we bring in on any given Sunday goes towards operational expenses for our ministries." God interrupts "Are you trying to justify your actions to me? Sit down and shut up with your diamond studded pinky ring and watch. I know you think I don't know about that backdoor deal you struck with those city officials, or that family you hurt when you fired that woman's husband based on a rumor that turned out to be a lie. All I am hearing are excuses. Not one of you has been able to justify your actions to me. Is it not enough that I have removed your honor and spread dung on your faces. Can't you see I have caused the people to no longer respect you? I have even tried to get your attention through your health, but you wouldn't listen. Here is my resolve to you wealthy leaders. Repent! Sell all that you have and give it to the struggling families in your churches, and I will drop the charges I have against you and you will have eternal life. Sell all that you have and give it to the poor and I will drop the charges I have against you and you will have eternal life. In addition to this get out from behind those four walls and get into the neighborhoods and show my people my love. Didn't I tell you that I have other sheep that must be brought into the fold? Well they are not coming to your buildings or your conferences, I meant for you to go to them. You should know better. Out of everybody on the planet, if anybody should know the difference between right and wrong it is you. You have caused my people to error and stray.

Here is my ruling, repent every one of you. Stop chasing wealth and hurting people. Get out of those buildings and go after my children who are lost. And have those ministers take those silly badges off, everybody already knows who they are. This court will convene again individually at a time of my choosing at the judgment seat of my Son. I suggest you use this time wisely. Right now I am not pleased with you. I will be watching and evaluating how you handle my business and my people over the next 20 years. If I do not like what I see, I will hold each of you accountable one by one and you will answer to me. Do not blow this time of repentance that I am giving you. This court is dismissed."

All Rise!

Malachi is perhaps the greatest book I have ever read on accountability. You do not have to read far to find that God has a real problem with how his leaders are handling the tithes and offerings the people entrusted into their hands. God has focused his attention on those who are in charge of leading his people. This is not simply an act of the divine speaking to leadership, so they in turn can straighten the people out. God is speaking directly to leadership in this instance, because they have aborted the plan of provision that God had entrusted to them.

(Deuteronomy 14:27-29) He is speaking to leadership because their actions are the root cause behind the people's struggles.

Many of the people were bringing what God had required. Granted they were not faithful, but the leaders were keeping the best of what was brought for themselves and giving God what was left. The system was corrupt and God had enough. To protect the integrity of rightly dividing the word and avoid exegetical incongruity, I have included the letter written by Malachi. The language used in *The Message: The Bible in Contemporary Language,* was truly inspiring to me. I believe it will inspire you to new insights just as it has done for me.

The Book of Malachi— Taken from The Message Bible

Malachi 1 (The Message)
Malachi 1
No More of This So-Called Worship!

[1]A Message. God's Word to Israel through Malachi: [2-3]God said, "I love you." You replied, "Really? How have you loved us?" "Look at history" (this is God's answer). "Look at how differently I've treated you, Jacob, from Esau: I loved Jacob and hated Esau. I reduced pretentious Esau to a molehill, turned his whole country into a ghost town."

[4]When Edom (Esau) said, "We've been knocked down, but we'll get up and start over, good as new," God-of-the-Angel-Armies said, "Just try it and see how far you get. When I knock you down, you stay down. People will take one look at you and say, 'Land of Evil!' and 'the God-cursed tribe!'

[5]"Yes, take a good look. Then you'll see how faithfully I've loved you and you'll want even more, saying, 'May GOD be even greater, beyond the borders of Israel!'

⁶"Isn't it true that a son honors his father and a worker his master? So if I'm your Father, where's the honor? If I'm your Master, where's the respect?" God-of-the-Angel-Armies is calling you on the carpet: "You priests despise me!

"You say, 'Not so! How do we despise you?'

"By your shoddy, sloppy, defiling worship.

"You ask, 'What do you mean, "defiling"? What's defiling about it?'

⁷⁻⁸"When you say, 'The altar of God is not important anymore; worship of God is no longer a priority,' that's defiling. And when you offer worthless animals for sacrifices in worship, animals that you're trying to get rid of—blind and sick and crippled animals—isn't that defiling? Try a trick like that with your banker or your senator—how far do you think it will get you?" God-of-the-Angel-Armies asks you.

⁹"Get on your knees and pray that I will be gracious to you. You priests have gotten everyone in trouble. With this kind of conduct, do you think I'll pay attention to you?" God-of-the-Angel-Armies asks you.

¹⁰"Why doesn't one of you just shut the Temple doors and lock them? Then none of you can get in and play at religion with this silly, empty-headed worship. I am not pleased. The God-of-the-Angel-Armies is not pleased. And I don't want any more of this so-called worship!

Offering God Something Hand-Me-Down, Broken, or Useless

¹¹"I am honored all over the world. And there are people who know how to worship me all over the world, who honor me by bringing their best to me. They're saying it everywhere: 'God is greater, this God-of-the-Angel-Armies.'

[12-13] *"All except you. Instead of honoring me, you profane me. You profane me when you say, 'Worship is not important, and what we bring to worship is of no account,' and when you say, 'I'm bored—this doesn't do anything for me.' You act so superior, sticking your noses in the air—act superior to me, God-of-the-Angel-Armies! And when you do offer something to me, it's a hand-me-down, or broken, or useless. Do you think I'm going to accept it? This is God speaking to you!*

[14] *"A curse on the person who makes a big show of doing something great for me—an expensive sacrifice, say—and then at the last minute brings in something puny and worthless! I'm a great king, God-of-the-Angel-Armies, honored far and wide, and I'll not put up with it!"*

Malachi 2 (The Message)
Malachi 2
Desecrating the Holiness of God

[1-3] *"And now this indictment, you priests! If you refuse to obediently listen, and if you refuse to honor me, God-of-the-Angel-Armies, in worship, then I'll put you under a curse. I'll exchange all your blessings for curses. In fact the curses are already at work because you're not serious about honoring me. Yes, and the curse will extend to your children. I'm going to plaster your faces with rotting garbage, garbage thrown out from your feasts. That's what you have to look forward to!*

[4-6] *"Maybe that will wake you up. Maybe then you'll realize that I'm indicting you in order to put new life into my covenant with*

the priests of Levi, the covenant of God-of-the-Angel-Armies. My covenant with Levi was to give life and peace. I kept my covenant with him, and he honored me. He stood in reverent awe before me. He taught the truth and did not lie. He walked with me in peace and uprightness. He kept many out of the ditch, kept them on the road.

7-9 "It's the job of priests to teach the truth. People are supposed to look to them for guidance. The priest is the messenger of God-of-the-Angel-Armies. But you priests have abandoned the way of priests. Your teaching has messed up many lives. You have corrupted the covenant of priest Levi. God-of-the-Angel-Armies says so. And so I am showing you up for who you are. Everyone will be disgusted with you and avoid you because you don't live the way I told you to live, and you don't teach my revelation truly and impartially."

10Don't we all come from one Father? Aren't we all created by the same God? So why can't we get along? Why do we desecrate the covenant of our ancestors that binds us together?

11-12Judah has cheated on God—a sickening violation of trust in Israel and Jerusalem: Judah has desecrated the holiness of God by falling in love and running off with foreign women, women who worship alien gods. God's curse on those who do this! Drive them out of house and home! They're no longer fit to be part of the community no matter how many offerings they bring to God-of-the-Angel-Armies.

13-15And here's a second offense: You fill the place of worship with your whining and sniveling because you don't get what you want from God. Do you know why? Simple. Because God was there as a witness when you spoke your marriage vows to your young bride, and now you've broken those vows, broken the faith-bond with your vowed companion, your covenant wife. God, not you, made marriage. His Spirit inhabits even the smallest details of marriage. And what does he want from marriage? Children of God, that's what. So guard the spirit of marriage within you. Don't cheat on your spouse.

[16] "I hate divorce," says the God of Israel. God-of-the-Angel-Armies says, "I hate the violent dismembering of the 'one flesh' of marriage." So watch yourselves. Don't let your guard down. Don't cheat.

[17] You make God tired with all your talk.

"How do we tire him out?" you ask.

By saying, "God loves sinners and sin alike. God loves all." And also by saying, "Judgment? God's too nice to judge."

Malachi 3 (The Message)
Malachi 3
The Master You've Been Looking For

[1] "Look! I'm sending my messenger on ahead to clear the way for me. Suddenly, out of the blue, the Leader you've been looking for will enter his Temple—yes, the Messenger of the Covenant, the one you've been waiting for. Look! He's on his way!" A Message from the mouth of God-of-the-Angel-Armies.

[2-4] But who will be able to stand up to that coming? Who can survive his appearance?

He'll be like white-hot fire from the smelter's furnace. He'll be like the strongest lye soap at the laundry. He'll take his place as a refiner of silver, as a cleanser of dirty clothes. He'll scrub the Levite priests clean, refine them like gold and silver, until they're fit for God, fit to present offerings of righteousness. Then, and only then, will Judah and Jerusalem be fit and pleasing to God, as they used to be in the years long ago.

⁵"Yes, I'm on my way to visit you with Judgment. I'll present compelling evidence against sorcerers, adulterers, liars, those who exploit workers, those who take advantage of widows and orphans, those who are inhospitable to the homeless—anyone and everyone who doesn't honor me." A Message from God-of-the-Angel-Armies. ⁶⁻⁷"I am God—yes, I Am. I haven't changed. And because I haven't changed, you, the descendants of Jacob, haven't been destroyed. You have a long history of ignoring my commands. You haven't done a thing I've told you. Return to me so I can return to you," says God-of-the-Angel-Armies.

"You ask, 'But how do we return?'

⁸⁻¹¹"Begin by being honest. Do honest people rob God? But you rob me day after day.

"You ask, 'How have we robbed you?'

"The tithe and the offering—that's how! And now you're under a curse —the whole lot of you—because you're robbing me. Bring your full tithe to the Temple treasury so there will be ample provisions in my Temple. Test me in this and see if I don't open up heaven itself to you and pour out blessings beyond your wildest dreams. For my part, I will defend you against marauders, protect your wheat fields and vegetable gardens against plunderers." The Message of God-of-the-Angel-Armies.

12 "You'll be voted 'Happiest Nation.' You'll experience what it's like to be a country of grace." God-of-the-Angel-Armies says so.

The Difference Between Serving God and Not Serving Him

13 God says, "You have spoken hard, rude words to me.

"You ask, 'When did we ever do that?'

14-15 "When you said, 'It doesn't pay to serve God. What do we ever get out of it? When we did what he said and went around with long faces, serious about God-of-the-Angel-Armies, what difference did it make? Those who take life into their own hands are the lucky ones. They break all the rules and get ahead anyway. They push God to the limit and get by with it.'"

16 Then those whose lives honored God got together and talked it over. God saw what they were doing and listened in. A book was opened in God's presence and minutes were taken of the meeting, with the names of the God-fearers written down, all the names of those who honored God's name.

17-18 God-of-the-Angel-Armies said, "They're mine, all mine. They'll get special treatment when I go into action. I treat them with the same consideration and kindness that parents give the child who honors them. Once more you'll see the difference it makes between being a person who does the right thing and one who doesn't, between serving God and not serving him."

These leaders had been disregarding the needs of God's people and stealing from Him for so long, that the people began to mirror their actions. He formally confronted their pious disregard for the positions they held. Their responses provide us with insights that they actually believed they were effectively casting the shadow of a leader. Instead of repenting they justified their actions. No thought had been given to caring for the elderly, widows, or fatherless as *Deuteronomy 14:29* instructed them to do. These priests made sure their own personal needs were met. It's frightening to think that you could be led by someone who is doing the wrong thing but really believes they are right. It is this principle reason that Israel was not able to be prosperous and experience the open window blessing promised. The leaders who represented Israel were in error, the people followed in this same error, and as a result God could not bless anyone.

No matter how much the people gave, God could not bless them because the leaders who represented them were raking it all into their own personal bank accounts.

Remember, the charge of robbery was spoken to the leaders; laity got looped in by association. If your leader is stealing the tithes and offerings, you have to decide if you are going to continue giving to that ministry or individual.

The verse below spells out the sentencing.

Malachi 3:8-9 (NLT)
⁸ Will a man rob God? Yet ye have robbed me. But ye say, Wherein have we robbed thee? In tithes and offerings.
⁹ Ye are cursed with a curse: for ye have robbed me, even this whole nation.

Remember, all those associated with the crooked leaders in the book of Malachi received the same verdict passed down to those leaders. They became accessories to the crime of robbery based on association and membership.

You may say that it does not matter what my leader does with the money as long as I bring it. After all, I'm not giving it to a man; I'm giving it to God. One of the problems is that it never reaches God! As a result the heavens become shut up and no blessings flow from the windows because the storehouse was improperly managed. . If they steal from God, they will steal from you. Read the charges again carefully because the charges are being brought against "a man," but the curse is pronounced against "the nation." It is a mistake to align yourself with a thief. When you do this, you become an accomplice who is guilty by association. I believe God attributed the actions of the priest to the entire nation because many of them sat in silence knowing what the priests were doing, but refused to hold the leaders accountable for their questionable actions. The people played dumb, and it cost them dearly. What is your silence costing you?

1. Many of the people brought what God asked of them, some of them did not.
2. The priest left God the worst of what was brought, keeping the best for himself.
3. God cursed the priest.
4. God cursed the people as a result of what the priest did because ultimately God never got what he asked for.

Everyone fell under the curse of God's judgment, and this could be linked directly to the priest's lifestyle of manipulation, mismanagement, and selfish greed. The silencing of the lambs had established itself as a stronghold in the lives of the people. Group think had taken over, and the whole nation had become a community church of enablers. Everyone saw what was happening. No one had the courage to break ranks and say enough is enough, something is wrong with this picture. They heard no evil, saw no evil and spoke no evil. Not even their own imperfections could excuse their silence. Maybe they were silent because they were afraid of being marked as controversial rebels who would not submit to leadership if they spoke out. Perhaps they did not want to be the subject of the sermon for the next four weeks. Could it be that they feared they would be thrown out and villianized. Maybe they thought to themselves, "Something isn't right, but I don't want to go against leadership, even though I know this leadership is dead wrong." Some would consider this to be a sign of weakness. If you are harboring these same feelings, I want to remind you of the words of the controversial Christ who is your leader.

St. Matthew 10:26-28 (KJV)
26Fear them not therefore: for there is nothing covered, that shall not be revealed; and hid, that shall not be known.
27What I tell you in darkness, that speak ye in light: and what ye hear in the ear, that preach ye upon the housetops.
28And fear not them which kill the body, but are not able to kill the soul: but rather fear him which is able to destroy both soul and body in hell.

Suffice to say that managing all the tithes and offerings that the people brought to the priest was no small undertaking. God was particular about how these were to be handled; the priest simply grew weary of doing it God's way. It was easier in the priest's eyes to bring God what was left as opposed to bringing Him what was right.

The book of Malachi is designed to shed light on the selfish acts of the leaders and the people they led. Somehow you have been made to believe this letter belongs exclusively to you, the church member. This is not your letter, and when you read it, you must understand it from that basis. The people were struggling daily before a closed window because of selfish leadership. Had God not said anything, who knows just how bad things might really have gotten? Fast forward three hundred years where we find Jesus standing in her courts. He kicked over tables and whipped them because they were converting and changing money for goods in the house of God. That is how bad things had gotten.

The next time someone tells you that you are robbing God after you have freely volunteered countless hours and given your best to God asking for nothing in return; I want you to take a look at the name tag contained in the collar of his/her suit. Take a look at the six-figure, his and hers cars, sitting on twenty-five inches of chrome they drove up in. Drive by the seven-figure homes where they lay their heads down at night, and if they would be truly transparent, take a look at their deposit statements and bank account balances. Compare all that they have to the needs of those who are members of their own ministries and ask yourself "Is there a thief in the house?"

CHAPTER 16

Where in God's Name Is the Beef?

In its commercial, which aired in 1984, Wendy's made an observation that many knew to be true but did not know how to express. Wendy's dared to ask the question of those leading the fast-food industry—such as McDonald's with its 31,000-plus locations and Burger King with it 12,000-plus locations compared to the significantly smaller Wendy's franchises with approximately 6,650 locations—am I really getting what I paid for?

The larger companies had taken in a great deal of cash, but Wendy's raised the question, "Where's the beef?" "Where's the beef?" resonated with the American population as we considered the size of the patty compared to the price we were being asked to pay. Wendy's dared to proclaim that we should be seeing more for our money, and by doing so, they raised the social awareness of the consumer that something was truly missing between the fluffy buns. Soon we began to realize that we were being given a lot of fluff in the form of the toasted bun but not much at all by way of real meat.

"I'm going to quit my job because God is calling me into full-time ministry".

How many well-meaning individuals have uttered these words but have not understood the "don't work, don't eat" principle?

These same individuals believe that they should live solely off the fleece that the sheep provide. They have created a system within the church designed to supply all their needs according to the riches in their members' bank accounts by way of tithes and offerings. Although many of them do not work, they live lavishly off the wool they sheer from their sheep, until they no longer need to depend on the sheep's wool. Once they have amassed a comfortable lifestyle, they boast about not taking any wool from the sheep that helped get them to that point in the first place.

I know many of you may say, "But my leader does not take a salary from the ministry." I guess not! His combined household income is upper six to seven figures of tax free money. What portion of this tax free income is your leader attempting to justify? Who do you think is buying all those books they are selling, non-church people? If your leader earns a significant, zip code-changing income from his/her own efforts but has a church filled with struggling members, how does one justify him/her living as such while those members lose their homes to foreclosure? Or die from sickness and disease because they cannot afford treatment? No amount of personal efforts on their part could ever justify them watching this happen to those they claim to love and lead. The sole purpose of bringing the tithes and offerings into the storehouse was to ensure there was provision (beef) for the people. Many leaders extract more and more from their members and contribute proportionately less from their own personal resources. Rising expenses related to ministry needs have left members asking "Hey, where in God's name is the beef?"

How does a leader who is worth that amount of money justify asking struggling families to give radically to help him build a building that he is ultimately going to put his name on and employ his entire family to work in? In 1517 a friar named Johaan Tetzel wanted to raise money to renovate the Basilica located in Rome known as St. Peter's Basilica. In his 95 Thesis Martin Luther asks, what prevented the pope who was exorbitantly wealthy from building the basilica with his own money instead of relying on the money of poor believers. It was a good question then and I will pose the same question today. **If your net worth is fast approaching upper six to seven figures tax free incomes, what prevents you from funding your own building projects, especially since you are going to put your name on the building? Why should struggling families who earn $50,000 collectively on an annual basis pay for a building in which they have no equity?** They do not own their own homes but are asked to pay for a building they spend limited time in on a weekly basis. This is not being a good steward of their finances. It could possibly be justifiable if those families were able to receive help when needed, but this is often not the case. If you find the need to preach on the contents of this book, start your sermon by answering the two previous questions first. Until you can answer these two questions for your members, you have not earned the right to refute any of the truth contained in these pages. If it takes so much money to spread the Gospel and you are a Gospel preacher, how about starting with a few of your own tax free dollars?

The apostle Paul models a very different example for leaders to live by:

2 Thessalonians 3:6-10 (NLT)
[6] And now, dear brothers and sisters, we give you this command in the name of our Lord Jesus Christ: Stay away from all believers

who live idle lives and don't follow the tradition they received from us.
⁷For you know that you ought to imitate us. We were not idle when we were with you.
⁸We never accepted food from anyone without paying for it. We worked hard day and night so we would not be a burden to any of you.
⁹We certainly had the right to ask you to feed us, but we wanted to give you an example to follow.
¹⁰Even while we were with you, we gave you this command: "Those unwilling to work will not get to eat."

He did not say we have a responsibility to care for those who were able to work. They can do that for themselves. Likewise if an individual is unable to work for a wage, this should not prevent him from doing some sort of work until the wage eventually follows. If an individual can work but chooses not to, Paul says that he has not earned the right to eat. Working and eating go hand in hand. The only thing I can think of that would be less appealing than a grown child who lives at home, stressing Mom and Dad out because he/she refuses to work, is a leader who serves in the house and fosters similar burdens on those he leads.

Consider the wisdom of Solomon from the book of Proverbs on this subject.

Proverbs 10:4 (NLT)
⁴ Lazy people are soon poor; hard workers get rich.

Proverbs 6:9-11 (NLT)
⁹ But you, lazybones, how long will you sleep? When will you wake up?
¹⁰ A little extra sleep, a little more slumber,
a little folding of the hands to rest—

¹¹ then poverty will pounce on you like a bandit;
scarcity will attack you like an armed robber.

In I Corinthians 9:3-18 (NLT), Paul teaches the following regarding preaching and money.

³This is my answer to those who question my authority.
⁴Don't we have the right to live in your homes and share your meals?
⁵Don't we have the right to bring a Christian wife with us as the other apostles and the Lord's brothers do, and as Peter does?
⁶Or is it only Barnabas and I who have to work to support ourselves?
⁷What soldier has to pay his own expenses? What farmer plants a vineyard and doesn't have the right to eat some of its fruit? What shepherd cares for a flock of sheep and isn't allowed to drink some of the milk?
⁸Am I expressing merely a human opinion, or does the law say the same thing?
⁹For the law of Moses says, "You must not muzzle an ox to keep it from eating as it treads out the grain." Was God thinking only about oxen when he said this?
¹⁰Wasn't he actually speaking to us? Yes, it was written for us, so that the one who plows and the one who threshes the grain might both expect a share of the harvest.
¹¹Since we have planted spiritual seed among you, aren't we entitled to a harvest of physical food and drink?
¹²If you support others who preach to you, shouldn't we have an even greater right to be supported? But we have never used this right. We would rather put up with anything than be an obstacle to the Good News about Christ.
¹³Don't you realize that those who work in the temple get their meals from the offerings brought to the temple? And those who serve at the altar get a share of the sacrificial offerings.

[14]In the same way, the Lord ordered that those who preach the Good News should be supported by those who benefit from it.
[15]Yet I have never used any of these rights. And I am not writing this to suggest that I want to start now. In fact, I would rather die than lose my right to boast about preaching without charge.
[16]Yet preaching the Good News is not something I can boast about. I am compelled by God to do it. How terrible for me if I didn't preach the Good News!
[17]If I were doing this on my own initiative, I would deserve payment. But I have no choice, for God has given me this sacred trust.
[18]What then is my pay? It is the opportunity to preach the Good News without charging anyone. That's why I never demand my rights when I preach the Good News.

In the book of Acts 4:32-35 (NLT), this local body of believers had unity and equity.

[32]All the believers were united in heart and mind. And they felt that what they owned was not their own, so they shared everything they had.
[33]The apostles testified powerfully to the resurrection of the Lord Jesus, and God's great blessing was upon them all.
[34]There were no needy people among them, because those who owned land or houses would sell them [35]and bring the money to the apostles to give to those in need.

It is important to understand that what we are looking at here is a system of provision that does not include tithing. What takes place here is significantly different from what we see taking place throughout the entire Old Testament.

What exactly was happening in the hearts and minds of the people that would make them behave in this way? They were completely sold out to God! Whatever they had in their possession, they made it all totally available to Him! They took the limits off to meet one another's needs. Any member who was in need could come to the leaders to whom the provisions were entrusted, and have their needs wiped out. If you were wondering how we would finance the efforts of the church, I would first say that the issue really is not about having finances for the church. The issue is more about the church doing something worth financing, something more than the pastor's anniversary. The church should be about the Father's business, and doing what God has called it to do for its members within. It should not overlook those who are without in the local community in which it has been planted—reaching out and significantly involving itself in the affairs of people, making life better for those around and within it. Any church that does this will find that the people within and without (businesses included) will open their hearts and their wallets to ensure every effort is undergirded monetarily. They may never say it, but the people in your church have a real issue when their house ends in foreclosure while the pastor buys another new car and he doesn't work anywhere.

The believers in the fourth chapter of the book of Acts sold what they had and gave all the proceeds from the sales to the preachers. The preachers received what was brought on the behalf of God. It was God's intent to give it back to the people so that no one lacked anything. This is the New Testament mirror of the "storehouse" spoken of in Malachi 3.

I call it "reciprocal giving." See chart A2, which demonstrates the cycle of giving.

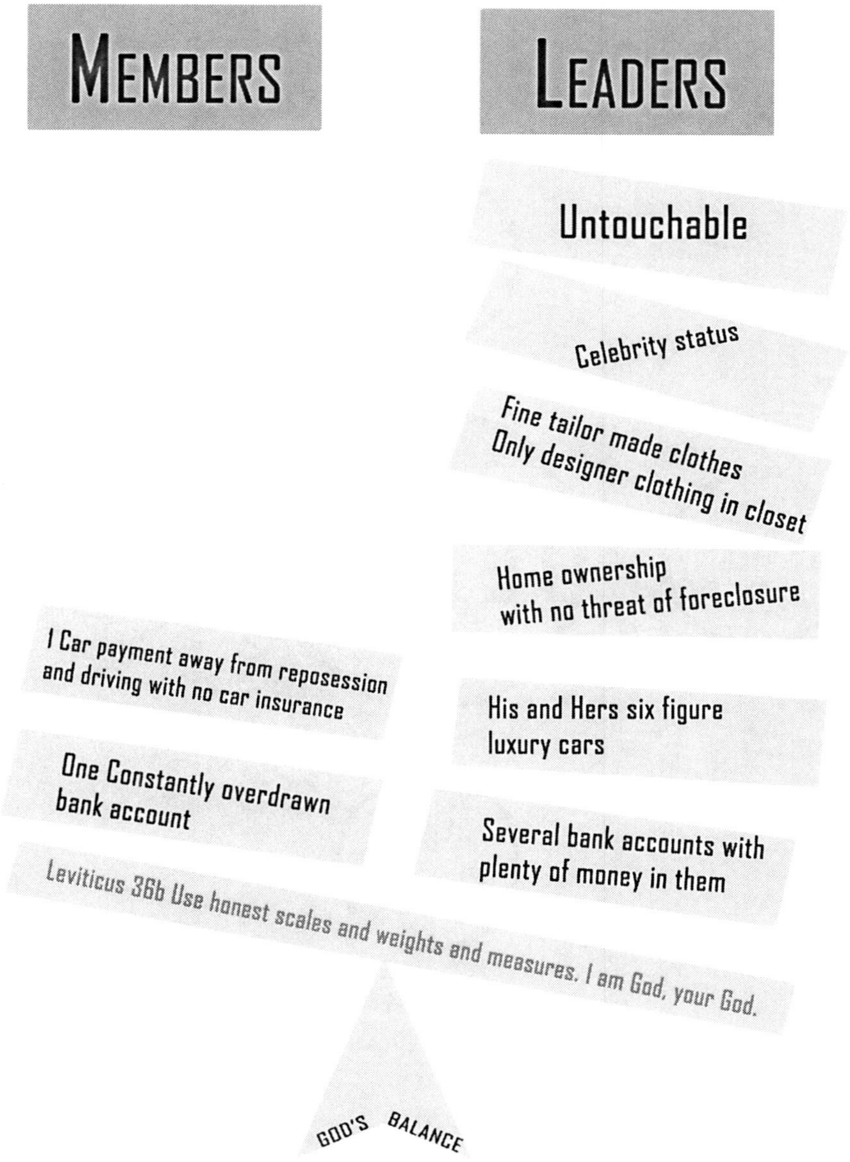

MEMBERS

LEADERS

Untouchable

Celebrity status

Fine tailor made clothes
Only designer clothing in closet

Home ownership
with no threat of foreclosure

1 Car payment away from reposession
and driving with no car insurance

His and Hers six figure
luxury cars

One Constantly overdrawn
bank account

Several bank accounts with
plenty of money in them

Leviticus 36b Use honest scales and weights and measures. I am God, your God.

GOD'S   BALANCE

[Chart A1]

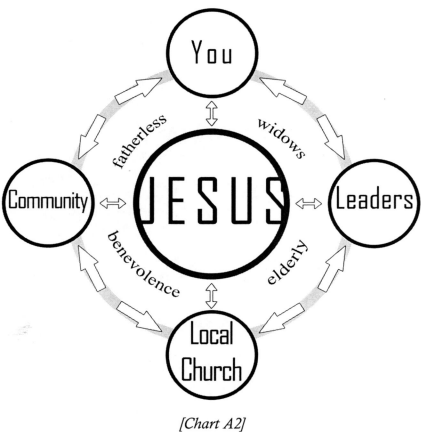

[Chart A2]
Cycle of Giving

This is how giving should look in the life of a believer irrespective of any titles held. Take a minute to analyze the chart. You will see that giving is cyclical. Every aspect of life is positively impacted by a healthy system that promotes systematic giving where everyone's needs are met. Christ sits at the heart of it all because he is the source and example of cyclical giving.

Jesus Christ gave his life for us and to us.

Take a look at another example of what giving should look like from God's perspective; it's truly eye opening.

2 Corinthians 8 (NLT)
A Call to Generous Giving

[1]Now I want you to know, dear brothers and sisters, what God in his kindness has done through the churches in Macedonia. [2]They are being tested by many troubles, and they are very poor. But they are also filled with abundant joy, which has overflowed in rich generosity.

[3]For I can testify that they gave not only what they could afford, but far more. And they did it of their own free will. [4]They begged us again and again for the privilege of sharing in the gift for the believers in Jerusalem. [5]They even did more than we had hoped, for their first action was to give themselves to the Lord and to us, just as God wanted them to do.

[6]So we have urged Titus, who encouraged your giving in the first place, to return to you and encourage you to finish this ministry of giving. [7]Since you excel in so many ways—in your faith, your gifted speakers, your knowledge, your enthusiasm,

and your love from us[c]—I want you to excel also in this gracious act of giving.

[8]I am not commanding you to do this. But I am testing how genuine your love is by comparing it with the eagerness of the other churches.

[9]You know the generous grace of our Lord Jesus Christ. Though he was rich, yet for your sakes he became poor, so that by his poverty he could make you rich.

[10]Here is my advice: It would be good for you to finish what you started a year ago. Last year you were the first who wanted to give, and you were the first to begin doing it. [11]Now you should finish what you started. Let the eagerness you showed in the beginning be matched now by your giving. Give in proportion to what you have. [12]Whatever you give is acceptable if you give it eagerly. And give according to what you have, not what you don't have. [13]Of course, I don't mean your giving should make life easy for others and hard for yourselves. I only mean that there should be some equality. [14]Right now you have plenty and can help those who are in need. Later, they will have plenty and can share with you when you need it. In this way, things will be equal. [15]As the Scriptures say,

"Those who gathered a lot had nothing left over, and those who gathered only a little had enough."

Titus and His Companions

[16]But thank God! He has given Titus the same enthusiasm for you that I have. [17]Titus welcomed our request that he visit you again. In fact, he himself was very eager to go and see you. [18]We

are also sending another brother with Titus. All the churches praise him as a preacher of the Good News. [19]He was appointed by the churches to accompany us as we take the offering to Jerusalem—a service that glorifies the Lord and shows our eagerness to help.

[20]We are traveling together to guard against any criticism for the way we are handling this generous gift. [21]We are careful to be honorable before the Lord, but we also want everyone else to see that we are honorable.

CHAPTER 17

Salvation Is Free

We are told that the piles of money being thrown on the altars of our churches are being used to spread the gospel. Remember it costs nothing to tell people about Jesus.

It costs money to be on the radio and television which are less effective than a face-to-face conversation with your neighbor, coworker, brother-in-law, children's principal, grocery store clerk, elderly at the senior citizens home, those confined to their sick beds in the hospitals, or those fifteen minutes away locked behind bars in prison. It costs less money to drive a few blocks to the nearest juvenile detention center and tell a lost and confused teenage girl about the saving grace of Jesus than it does to pay my share of a one-hour television broadcast, which airs during prime time five nights a week. Have we not considered that the only ones watching Christian television are Christians? If we really want to make good use of our wool, secular airwaves is a good place to knit our blankets of warmth, love, and care.

The following graph depicts the financial life cycle of the church, the leader, and the member.

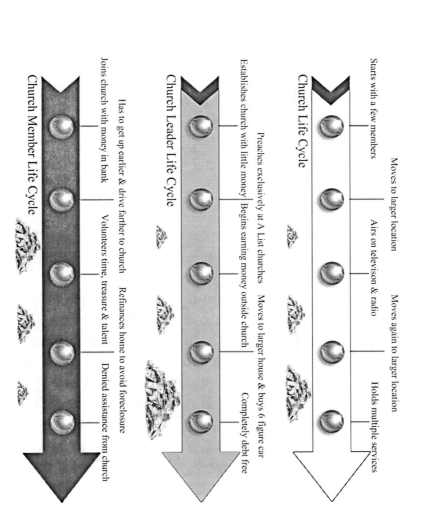

Church Life Cycle

Starts with a few members

Moves to larger location

Moves again to larger location

Airs on televison & radio

Holds multiple services

Church Leader Life Cycle

Establishes church with little money

Preaches exclusively at A List churches

Begins earning money outside church

Moves to larger house & buys 6 figure car

Completely debt free

Church Member Life Cycle

Joins church with money in bank

Has to get up earlier & drive farther to church

Volunteers time, treasure & talent

Refinances home to avoid foreclosure

Denied assistance from church

CHAPTER 18

Uncle!

It's a weird sounding word, isn't it? Say it under your breath where only you can hear it. It sounds like a word that a baby would use when he/she is first learning to talk. We all know what it describes. I do not want to talk about uncle in the traditional sense—the brother of one's father or mother. Let me explain. As a child I grew up in the inner city of Buffalo, New York. Growing up there meant you had to be smart and tough. I have tremendous respect for those who were raised in inner cities across this great country. If you can face all the challenges that go along with inner-city living and still make it, you are a survivor. Surviving the ghetto meant you had to have street smarts. It's hard to explain exactly what that means if you have never had to use them just to survive. It's an inner knowing, a heightened sense of awareness of one's surroundings. We knew a phony from the real deal when we saw one. This inner knowing was developed at an early age growing up in the city.

I can remember having to fight all the time as a kid. Sometimes I was scared, but as the physical altercations continued, my toughness grew and my fears subsided. I had an older cousin who was small in stature, but man was he tough. He wasn't afraid of anything or anyone. He was fearless. He was small, but he was tough physically, and more importantly he was tough mentally. He was the kind of kid who, when my aunty gave him a whippin', he did not cry. I couldn't believe it! Watching him taking a very deliberate whippin'—sometimes with an extension cord, metal hanger, one of those orange Hot Wheels racing car tracks, or a leather belt without shedding one tear—would often-times leave me standing there with my mouth open. No matter what anyone dished out to him, he could take it.

We called him Little James. As long as I live, I will never forget the life lessons he taught me growing up as a kid, one of which was how to write my name. Although I didn't know it at the time, God was using him to teach me something far more valuable than how to legibly string a few letters together. He taught me how to fight. I'm not speaking purely of physical defense, because that part I had to learn in real time. I can re-member on several occasions wrestling with him. He would pin me down and put me in a headlock and squeeze. He would laugh and antagonize me as he held me down and say, "What you gonna do?" as he antagonistically licked my face. "You gonna cry like a baby and quit, or are you gonna get up?" He was re-lentless. "You want your momma, don't you, boy?" There were times when he held on so long that I could tell he was tired. "Say uncle! Say uncle!" He would shout. After lying there under his impenetrable grip, I knew when I had been beaten. When I could not take any more, I cried "Uncle!" He would laugh as he refused to let me go. "Get up, punk." "Awe, you gonna cry like a baby?" I couldn't tell at that time what I clearly understand now. He wasn't' trying to hurt me; he was trying to teach me.

As much as I minded being held down against my will, it was nothing compared to being called something I knew I was not. The struggle was teaching me that freedom does not come without a fight. It was this belief that began to fuel the toughness within me. I'm not suggesting that if a man cries it is a sign of weakness. I am human and hurt just like anybody else. Nonetheless, I was the product of a "hard knocks" life environment, and no one was going to make me feel like I was a loser, a quitter. Those encounters helped me to quickly learn how to dig down deep and survive in what seemed like a no-win situation. I would fight back so hard until I began digging my fingernails into any of his body parts that were visible. I would writhe out of control to loosen his grip, and yes, I would bite him anywhere my teeth could find fresh meat. I can remember my head and ears being bruised red as I did whatever it took to break free from his vice-grip headlocks. It's important that you know he never *let* me go. I would always have to find a way to break free and get up. Sometimes his attacks would come out of nowhere, but I learned early that there were no rules in a real fight, and you have to do whatever it takes to get someone off you. Little did I know, God was using my cousin to build a strong foundation of never saying uncle, "to get up no matter what" into my mental makeup.

How does this story fit into the discussion at hand? I'm glad you asked.

In this financial system of control, don't expect imbalanced leaders to let you go. You have to do whatever it takes to get free from their onslaught of conmanlation.
Never cry uncle!

CHAPTER 19

One for the Money, Two for the Show

I can remember the day when the preachers would travel from city to city conducting revivals. There were small storefront revivals, and then there were citywide ones as well. There would be so many people packed into that small church that the walls would literally sweat. If you were fortunate, there would be a big, noisy, round-shaped fan doing its best to cool the place but to no avail. For all its efforts to cool us off, all it could do was blow around the hot air that had already engulfed the small room filled with hot, sweaty, fanning church people.

When the spirit of God hit the house, we called it "having a high time in the Lord." The women would be shouting and crying under the power of God, and the men would run all around the church. The preacher would be laying hands. I can still see that sister who had the devil cast out of her. Man, what power the church had back then! You could see a difference in her as she staggered to her feet with her eyes closed, repeatedly saying, "Thank you, Jesus; thank you, Jesus!" It was real. Every night would end with an altar call, and the preacher would call for those who wanted to be filled with the Holy Ghost.

They would come, and within minutes of praying on the altar, they would be so overwhelmed by the spirit that they began to speak in unknown tongues. I witnessed this with my own eyes. It was not manufactured, and the preacher did not have to conduct a song and dance to usher in God's presence. It was genuine. It was real. Sometimes the revivals were held under big white tents. Man, you could hear the sound of deliverance for miles, long before you actually reached the tent itself.

The choir would be singing, and the minister would be preaching under the anointing, and people would come from what seemed like every direction. I can remember witnessing winos staggering in off the streets and being hit by the undeniable power of God and leaving sober. Without a flyer or commercial, the Holy Spirit would pack them in, and people would be slain by the spirit, leaving the revival drunken in the spirit and delivered from their sins. This kind of service is hard to find nowadays as the compromising church of today is cooling off and loosing her power. We need those who know the way to stand forth and lead the way.

In the book of Acts 8, a man named Simon witnessed this same kind of service taking place, and he wanted it so badly that he was willing to spare no expense to get it, no matter the cost. Let's take a look at the account as recorded in the book of Acts:

Acts 8:14-23 (NLT)
14 When the apostles in Jerusalem heard that the people of Samaria had accepted God's message, they sent Peter and John there
15 As soon as they arrived, they prayed for these new believers to receive the Holy Spirit
16 The Holy Spirit had not yet come upon any of them, for they had only been baptized in the name of the Lord Jesus.
17 Then Peter and John laid their hands upon these believers, and they received the Holy Spirit.
18 When Simon saw that the Spirit was given when the apostles laid

their hands on people, he offered them money to buy this power.
[19]"Let me have this power, too," he exclaimed, "so that when I lay
my hands on people, they will receive the Holy Spirit!"
[20]But Peter replied, "May your money be destroyed with you for
thinking God's gift can be bought!
[21]You can have no part in this, for your heart is not right with God.
[22]Repent of your wickedness and pray to the Lord. Perhaps he will
forgive your evil thoughts, [23]for I can see that you are full of bitter
jealousy and are held captive by sin."

He thought that if he spent enough money, he could get the
Holy Spirit to move on his behalf. He wanted to do what they did,
but he went about it the wrong way. He wanted what they had,
but he did not want to go through what they had gone through
in order to be empowered to be used by God the way they were
being used. He had the wrong understanding about the relationship between God and money. He did not understand that God
cannot be influenced by money.

Years ago, there was an unspoken understanding among
everyone who parted the sacred text that "What I am doing is
not about me." I can still hear the preacher praying, "Lord, hide
me behind the cross; let no flesh be glorified in your sight." He
would continue, "Let your word speak through me, that your
people hear you and not me." He would conclude his prayer with
"Now, Lord, I decrease that you might increase. Get the glory
out of this service. Amen." Man, how I miss this kind of preacher! Where have they all gone? Have they all died off? Is there no
one standing in the gap, seeking the old paths of righteousness
where the only star in our service is the Bright and Morning Star,
the Lord Jesus Christ? Or have we all traded our black robes in
for new ones, complete with glitter, trimmed with our insignia
proudly embroidered across the arms and chest?

Starstruck! That's what comes to mind when one considers

the glory associated with many of today's "esteemed" men and women of the cloth. It's hard to believe that we have been deceived into believing there are "top" preachers. I was always taught that the focus is not the messenger but the message that he or she carries. It did not take many up-and-coming preachers long to figure out that, if you work it the right way, there is a great deal of money to be made in the preaching field. The oratorical gift has that innate ability to captivate and inspire the hearer to the point of enamored attraction. If the motives are not checked this gift can quickly turn into blind ambition.

Simon Magus, the magician in the book of Acts who tried to buy the power of miracles, should remind us that we have a responsibility to seek and to save that which is lost and guard our hearts from the love of money, which is the root to all evil. He thought his money could open doors for him. Paul says in

Hebrews 13:5 (NLT)
"Don't love money; be satisfied with what you have. For God has said, "I will never fail you. I will never abandon you."

I Timothy 6: 10 (NLT)
"For the love of money is the root of all kinds of evil. And some people, craving money, have wandered from the true faith and pierced themselves with many sorrows."

God will continue to bless you if you don't tithe. Remember, Galatians 3:9 says, all who put their faith in Christ share the same blessing Abraham received because of his faith. Your ability to receive in life is in direct alignment with your generosity. You must make the commitment to be an avid giver. You will not go to hell if you do not tithe. You will not be cursed if you do not tithe. Anyone who tells you differently does not fully understand tithes. Share what you know or gift them with a copy of *Sunday Morning Stickup*.

CHAPTER 20

Take God Out of the "Elaborate" Box

**No matter how much or how little your church costs,
God does not dwell there.**

L et me explain.

After Moses led the Exodus around 1450 BC, God appeared to him and gave him specific instructions for building the tabernacle. Look at the scripture below, and see if you can answer specifically why he wanted Moses to build it. *(See answer key in back of the book)*

Genesis 25:8-9 (NLT)
[8] *"Have the people of Israel build me a holy sanctuary so I can live among them.*
[9] *You must build this Tabernacle and its furnishings exactly according to the pattern I will show you."*

Multiple choice—circle the correct answer.
God instructed Moses to build the tabernacle because...

A. Moses had a desire to build it for God.
B. The people wanted a church home.
C. God wanted to live (dwell) among his people.
D. The people needed a place to worship.

The temple that Solomon built in 957 BC replaced the temporary tabernacle of the days of Moses that I just mentioned. God moved his residence from a temporary tent to a temporary building. See chart A3

I Kings 8:10-11 (NLT)
¹⁰When the priests came out of the Holy Place, a thick cloud filled the Temple of the LORD
¹¹The priests could not continue their service because of the cloud, for the glorious presence of the LORD filled the Temple.

God moved in with his people and agreed to stay under one condition: that they remain faithful to Him. He lived with them. His room was located in the Holy of Holies. He manifested himself to his people in what was called "Shekinah glory." It means to dwell or settle. It was not His ideal living arrangement. He wanted more. He really wanted to live in them, but this arrangement would do for now. His presence could be found in the temple.

This did not last long because the people did not have God in their hearts. God threatened to leave because of their continual backslidings. They were not faithful to Him at all. As a result of their idolatry, He turned them over to their enemies, and many of them were taken captive into foreign lands beginning with Assyria and then Babylon. Finally, under the Babylonian leader Nebuchadnezzar, God allowed them to be taken away captive. The people were taken away, and God's presence left the temple for good. In 586 BC, Nebuchadnezzar actually burned God's house to the ground. The temple was completely destroyed. The only reason Nebuchadnezzar was successful in doing this is because God had left the bad relationship he had with his people and moved out permanently, vowing never to return to that house again!

2 Kings 25:8-10 (NLT)
⁸On August 14 of that year, which was the nineteenth year of King Nebuchadnezzar's reign, Nebuzaradan, the captain of the guard and an official of the Babylonian king, arrived in Jerusalem.
⁹He burned down the Temple of the LORD, the royal palace, and all the houses of Jerusalem. He destroyed all the important buildings in the city.
¹⁰Then he supervised the entire Babylonian army as they tore down the walls of Jerusalem on every side.

While they were in Babylonian captivity, they had no physical place to worship God. His presence was gone. They were so homesick that they turned three times a day to face Jerusalem to pray in that direction. Up until this time, God's presence did not dwell within men. He dwelt in the temple. No temple for them meant no presence of God.

True or False (Circle your answer)

T F   God's glorious presence filled the temple that Solomon built for him.

T F   God lived with his people.

T F   God's presence could be found in the hearts of his people.

T F   Solomon's Temple where God lived was burned to the ground.

Many years later, around 538 BC under the leadership of Nehemiah, the children of Israel began rebuilding the temple from the charred stones that Nebuchadnezzar had left behind. Amazingly the stones used to rebuild the temple were actually the same ones that burned from the original building. The second most significant thing is that after they completed the rebuilding project, the Ark of the Covenant, which was a wooden box overlaid with gold, was not in the newly rebuilt temple. This is important because this is where the Shekhinah glory presence of God settled. Needless to say, the house of God would never be the same again. It would never be the same again because, although they rebuilt the physical building, they did not have God's physical presence. In this single act, God demonstrated his lack of desire to be contained within any box of any kind ever again. God has no desire to fill a building. His only desire has always been to fill you with His spirit which is His presence.

Acts 2:17 (KJV)
And it shall come to pass in the last days, saith God, I will pour out of my Spirit upon all flesh: and your sons and your daughters shall prophesy, and your young men shall see visions, and your old men shall dream dreams...

Consider this, many of our brothers and sisters live in countries that are not God friendly. Building a church is unthinkable. Attempting to do so would result in their deaths. They understand experientially that God's building project has nothing to do with brick and mortar. The building of the church is within.

If what I have just explained makes sense, I want to ask for another commitment from you. I want to ask that you commit to allowing him to fill your life to the extent that His presence dwells profoundly in you, and in all that you do. What do I mean? Throughout your day acknowledge Him with a quiet prayer by asking this simple question, "What would you have me do in this situation?" This is what I mean by giving Him access to dwell profoundly in you. Thank you for your commitment and dedication. I believe with all my heart that as you seek Him, His will for your life will become clearer as the years go by.

In 70 AD Titus destroyed the temple which was God's former house (it later became known as Herod's Temple) and carried all its vessels to Rome. He did not take the Ark of the Covenant because it was not there. Today the physical structure where Solomon's Temple once sat is now an Islamic temple called the Temple Mount. The significance of this is that God never intended to return to live in any structure that could be destroyed by men ever again. He sought a more permanent, eternal dwelling place. That place would be within the spirits of men. God is not in your church, He is in you and I. We are the church.

Ephesians 2:20-22(KJV)
20 And are built upon the foundation of the apostles and prophets, Jesus Christ himself being the chief corner stone;
21 In whom all the building fitly framed together groweth unto an holy temple in the Lord:
22 In whom ye also are builded together for an habitation of God through the Spirit.

If God no longer lives in the physical building where we congregate for three to four hours at a time on a weekly basis, could it be that we have misunderstood the purpose that we are to fulfill in seeing the whole earth filled with his presence? Could it be that He does not want us to bring the people within our four walls, but that He wants us to take His presence beyond those walls and manifest Him to the world in the same way that Christ did? Is it plausible that we have successfully contained within our boxes an uncontainable God who has no desire to be boxed in? If we want to be aligned to the instructions given to us in the great commission, we must not invite them; we have to go after them.

Mark 16:15 (KJV)
15 And he said unto them, Go ye into all the world, and preach the gospel to every creature.

If his presence is no longer in these physical structures that we put *man-made denominational* names on, then why do we continue to build them bigger in His name? The giving from members to build these boxes at times amounts to an astounding fifty, sixty, seventy, and even as much as ninety million dollars per structure? That doesn't include the cost to operate and maintain them.

To help better illustrate how God moved from one dwelling place to the next until he found in us an eternal resting place, see chart A3.

When it was adopted into the Mosaic Law, tithes were used to care for people not structures. In addition to other payments, Moses instituted an annual half-shekel payment for the upkeep of the temple structure, which each Jewish male from twenty years of age upward in Israel had to pay yearly. (Exodus 30:11–16) The temple was funded through a once-a-year offering. God's focus has always been you. Today we collect tithes to pay for a house that God has no investment, interest, and in many cases, presence in. As a master builder, before he laid the foundation of this planet deep within the earth, He drafted the blueprints for a building project to which Solomon's Temple would never compare.

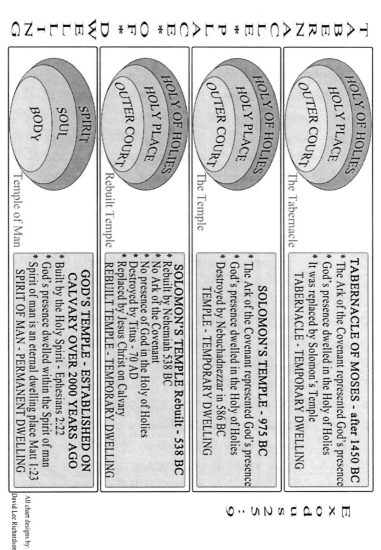

TABERNACLE
HOLY OF HOLIES
HOLY PLACE
OUTER COURT
The Tabernacle

TABERNACLE OF MOSES - after 1450 BC
* The Ark of the Covenant represented God's presence
* God's presence dwelled in the Holy of Holies
* It was replaced by Solomon's Temple
TABERNACLE - TEMPORARY DWELLING

Exodus 25:9

EZRA
HOLY OF HOLIES
HOLY PLACE
OUTER COURT
The Temple

SOLOMON'S TEMPLE - 975 BC
* The Ark of the Covenant represented God's presence
* God's presence dwelled in the Holy of Holies
* Destroyed by Nebuchadnezzar in 586 BC
TEMPLE - TEMPORARY DWELLING

CALL
HOLY OF HOLIES
HOLY PLACE
OUTER COURT
Rebuilt Temple

SOLOMON'S TEMPLE Rebuilt - 538 BC
* Rebuilt by Nehemiah 538 BC
* No Ark of the Covenant
* No presence of God in the Holy of Holies
* Destroyed by Titus - 70 AD
* Replaced by Jesus Christ on Calvary
REBUILT TEMPLE - TEMPORARY DWELLING

DWELLING
SPIRIT
SOUL
BODY
Temple of Man

GOD'S TEMPLE - ESTABLISHED ON CALVARY OVER 2000 YEARS AGO
* Built by the Holy Spirit - Ephesians 2:22
* God's presence dwelled within the Spirit of man
* Spirit of man is an eternal dwelling place Matt 1:23
SPIRIT OF MAN - PERMANENT DWELLING

[Chart A3]

All chart designs by:
David Lee Richardson

The blueprint to God's masterpiece was you. You are the ultimate building project that God has spared no expense to erect. Christ paid God the tithe of his life when he died on your behalf to pay for the entire venture. God is using that pure, undefiled tithe to care for and build *you*.

2 Corinthians 5:1-2 (NLT)
[1] "For we know that when this earthly tent we live in is taken down (that is, when we die and leave this earthly body), we will have a house in heaven, an eternal body made for us by God himself and not by human hands. [2] We grow weary in our present bodies, and we long to put on our heavenly bodies like new clothing."

It should be abundantly clear to you now that God does not need your money for the reasons that you have been told. No matter how opulent the church is, God does not want to dwell in a box. He wants to dwell in you. Does it really take forty-five million dollars to spread the gospel? You are the only house that God is interested in building, and Jesus has paid it all to make that possible. It costs you nothing to tell others about the saving grace of Jesus. That kind of money could ensure that no child goes hungry ever again in life. If you had forty-five to ninety million dollars and you could not give it to your leader, build a church, buy a mansion, or purchase a private jet, what would you do with it? Well, I want to encourage you to start doing "it" on the level where you are with what you currently have. You will find that you can accomplish those things with far less than the multiplied millions you think you have to have. What you have may not seem like much. But I want to challenge you to start where you are right now, and allow your Heavenly Father to work modern day miracles through your seemingly insuperable limitations.

You can do it because *you have Him in you*.

Conclusion

T he apostle Paul says it best in his letter to the church at Ephesus regarding God's eternal dwelling plan for you and me.

Ephesians 2:14-22 (NLT)
[14]For Christ himself has brought peace to us. He united Jews and Gentiles into one people when, in his own body on the cross, he broke down the wall of hostility that separated us. [15]He did this by ending the system of law with its commandments and regulations. He made peace between Jews and Gentiles by creating in himself one new people from the two groups. [16]Together as one body, Christ reconciled both groups to God by means of his death on the cross, and our hostility toward each other was put to death.
[17]He brought this Good News of peace to you Gentiles who were far away from him, and peace to the Jews who were near. [18]Now all of us can come to the Father through the same Holy Spirit because of what Christ has done for us.

A Temple for the Lord

[19] So now you Gentiles are no longer strangers and foreigners. You are citizens along with all of God's holy people. You are members of God's family. [20] Together, we are his house, built on the foundation of the apostles and the prophets. And the cornerstone is Christ Jesus himself. [21] We are carefully joined together in him, becoming a holy temple for the Lord. [22] Through him you Gentiles are also being made part of this dwelling where God lives by his Spirit.

You do not need money to build God a church. He never asked anyone to build one for Him in the first place (Matthew: 6 17-18). So what is your responsibility concerning responding to what you now know? The content of this book can be summed up in eight simple truths, which are listed below.

- Pursue God not money.
- If you have money, don't let money change you.
- Understand that no matter how much money you give (even sacrificially), you cannot pay for God's blessings.
- Always put the needs of people above the need for money.
- It costs you nothing to tell someone the story about what Jesus did for them. It costs them their soul if you do not.
- Do not be afraid to speak the truth.
- Remember that God does not want one-tenth of what you have; he really wants 100 percent of you.
- Understand that no matter how elaborate it is, God does not want to live in a box, he wants to live in you.

Literary Allegory:
"I've been feeling ill for quite some time now," said the wise old owl to his companion. "Maybe it's something you ate," she replied as he leaned over and belched out a butterfly.

Answer Key:
Multiple Choice Question – C
True/False Questions – T, T, F, T

CPSIA information can be obtained at www.ICGtesting.com
Printed in the USA
LVOW07s0846190813

348453LV00001B/1/P